A LITTLE BREEZE TO THE WEST

A LITTLE BREEZE TO THE WEST

ADVENTURES OF A YOUNG MAN'S SINGLE-HANDED VOYAGE TO HAWAII ON HIS 15-FT MONTGOMERY SAILBOAT

MICHAEL SCOTT MANN

Copyright © 2015 by Michael Scott Mann

A Little Breeze To The West

All rights reserved. No part of this book may be reproduced or transmitted in any form or by any means, electronic or mechanical, including photocopying, recording, or by any information storage and retrieval system without the written permission of the author, except where permitted by law.

The information in this book is meant to supplement, not replace, proper seamanship. Like any sport involving speed, equipment, balance and environmental factors, sailing poses some inherent risk. The author and publisher advise readers to take full responsibility for their safety and know their limits. Before practicing the skills described in this book, be sure that your equipment is well maintained, and do not take risks beyond your level of experience, aptitude, training, and comfort level.

Cover Photo: *Little Breeze's* maiden voyage around Catalina Island. Photo taken by Marc Hightower, Owner & Operator of Sky High Air Tours, Sevierville, TN.

Interior and Cover Design by Emily Weiss

Interior graphics by Michael and Laurie Mann

Audio tape conversion by Rich Estes

Montgomery 15 Original Brochure, Montgomery Marine, 935 W. 18th Street, Costa Mesa. CA: Permission granted by Jerry Montgomery

"I am not afraid of storms,
for I am learning how to sail my ship."

-Louisa May Alcott

DEDICATION

Janis L. Mann

In loving memory of my mom, who loved me enough to allow me to pursue my dream.

And my friend Marc Hightower, whose inspiration and expertise made this adventure possible

ACKNOWLEDGEMENTS

With loving thanks to my wife Laurie for believing in me and my story and for her encouragement and prodding to get this book published.

Thanks to my dear cousins Jody and Lloyd Bond for their enthusiastic editing and encouragement.

I also thank my friend John McDermott for his sound nautical advice.

Much appreciation to both Mel and Jane Mermelstein for cheering me on.

And special thanks to Jerry Montgomery for his invaluable experience and his fine tuning on the makings of a Montgomery sailboat.

CONTENTS

1. The Idea - Marc's Dream	*3*
2. The Boat - Little Breeze	*9*
3. Me - The Apprentice	*13*
4. Breaking the News to Family and Friends	*17*
5. Practice and Preparation	*21*
6. Putting It All Together	*33*
7. Let The Voyage Begin	*41*
8. Disappointing First Days	*49*
9. Settling Into A Routine	*59*
10. Baffling Winds	*71*
11. Becalmed - What Do I Do Now?	*87*
12. We've Hit The Trades	*101*
13. Ships That Pass In The Night	*113*
14. Halfway - My Point of No Return	*137*
15. Damage Control	*153*
16. Running Under Bare Pole	*167*
17. Unexpected Knockdown	*183*
18. We Read You Broken and Weak	*193*
19. What Island Is This?	*201*
20. What Happens Next?	*215*
Epilogue	*225*
Appendix I	*231*
Appendix II	*237*
Appendix III	*239*
Appendix IV	*241*
Glossary of Nautical Terms	*243*

Introduction

Here I am again, attempting to write the story of my solo sailing adventure from Huntington Beach, California to Hawaii, the summer of 1982, on my little sailboat affectionately, named *Little Breeze*. This is the second time I have tried to write down these experiences. My first attempt was during the first couple of years following my voyage, but I got caught up with life and returned to college so I put the book on hold. Fast forward thirty-three years and now my loving wife Laurie, is encouraging me to write and publish my story. She thinks it will be of interest to adventurous budding sailors wondering if they too can really accomplish their dreams. My only regret is that when the book is published, my mom, who died in 2008, will not be here to share in it. She would be proud, but she was always proud of "her boy," and she had the courage to let me go. So, here I go again on another of my many attempts and rewrites. I would really like to be fair to myself and to the story. With many years and many miles under the keel, the memories are starting to become fuzzy. I do have logs and journals that I kept during the voyage, I will use them to present the facts. Then I will fill in the rest of the story.

In my Sailing Log I recorded time, boat's position,

INTRODUCTION

course, speed, apparent wind speed/direction, sea state, and relevant notes. My Personal Journal is where I wrote down the day's accounts and events. And the recorded Audio Tape Journal is my verbal account of the day's happenings.

In March of 1982, I started fixing up my fifteen-foot sailboat, manufactured by Montgomery Marine Products of Costa Mesa, California, for a voyage that she was never designed for. After all, the Montgomery 15 was a lightweight fiberglass, trailerable, keel/centerboard pocket sloop meant for rivers, lakes, and protected waters (see brochure on pages 6-8). No one, except for my good friend Marc Hightower, could envision the boat sailing across a very rough Pacific Ocean. I got caught up in Marc's excitement and enthusiasm and decided that I would go for it! So with his help and technical advice I started to refit this little fiberglass daysailer to withstand the assaults of an open ocean crossing. After three months of preparations, and I could have kept tinkering endlessly; I set a date to depart, June 11, 1982.

CHAPTER ONE

THE IDEA - MARC'S DREAM

This whole adventure started March of 1982, in the 5th Street Tavern in Huntington Beach, California. I think today all the businesses in this area have been demolished, with new luxury condominiums having taken their place. Marc and I were renting his sister Laura's house nearby and decided, since it was Friday night, we would head over to 5th Street Tavern for a beer.

As the night progressed I remember Marc and I sitting at a table writing down ideas and notes on bar napkins, sketching out what it would take to get a Montgomery 15 ready to sail to Hawaii. These ideas included numerous modifications to improve the Montgomery's seaworthiness and livability, as well as making her easier to be sailed single-handed. This whole plan was Marc's idea from the beginning and I was basically going along for the ride, expect that it was my boat and I would be alone. We were intense in our discussions and as I look back this was a pivotal night for me—a night that forever changed my life and my destiny. Again, sailing a Montgomery 15 to Hawaii was Marc's dream that I would live out and make my own. That is why I am dedicating this

CHAPTER ONE

book not only to my mom but to Marc as well.

So before I tell you about myself, I have to introduce Marc Hightower. You might say that he was a typical kid from Southern California, long, straight, blond hair, blue eyes, five feet eight, medium build, and he loved the water. He loved surfing and sailing. In 1976, Marc even paddled a surfboard from San Pedro to Catalina Island, some twenty-six miles off Los Angeles. I met Marc back in 1974. We were attending high school, a boarding school, called the Catalina Island School nestled in Toyon Bay on Catalina Island. Marc was a junior and I was a sophomore when we met. It was here in this beautiful, semi-desert, island setting that Marc and another friend, Greg Sage, gave me my first real sailing lessons. I remember I really didn't like sailing because sailboats were slow compared to power boats, at the mercy of the wind, and *wet*. Marc and I spent a lot of time together at school and when we were home for holidays and summer vacations. He lived in Huntington Beach and I lived close-by in Fountain Valley. Marc often took me sailing on his twenty-two-foot ketch, affectionately called *Ketch 22* that he had docked in Dana Point, California. In time, I learned the basics and grew to thoroughly enjoy the challenge of sailing.

Originally, it was Marc who wanted to be the first to single-handedly circumnavigate the globe in a boat as small as fifteen feet. As the shop foreman for Jerry Montgomery, a boat builder, he was in charge of assembling different Montgomery Marine products and had a lot of time to dream and plan for his voyage and how he would accomplish it. Marc had helped design and build the molds for the new Montgomery 15 and Jerry gave Marc one of the first boats in lieu of payment for his extra help. Marc decided that he would need more room for the provisions and equipment needed for such a long trip, so he chose to sell his Montgomery 15 and buy a Montgomery 17. Guess who he sold the M-15 to-yep, me! I bought Marc's Montgomery 15 (which hadn't even been built yet) from him in February of 1981. I think the price was around $2,500 but it could have been more after all of the extras were added.

When my boat was being built, Marc still had in his mind that this boat was destined to travel, so he made many modifications for me just so I might be able to safely sail to Catalina someday. Little did either of us realize at the time where this boat would finally end up. Since Marc had access to the shop we took our time assembling my boat nights and weekends after work. It was routine for Marc to put a boat together in two or three days, but with the numerous upgrades, we took almost two months to build the boat.

Original 80's brochure

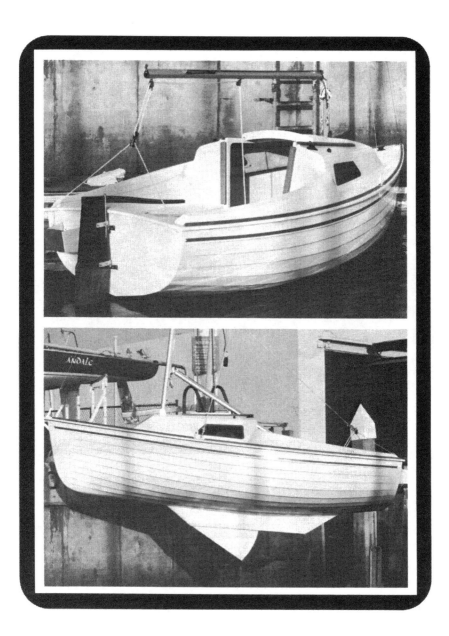

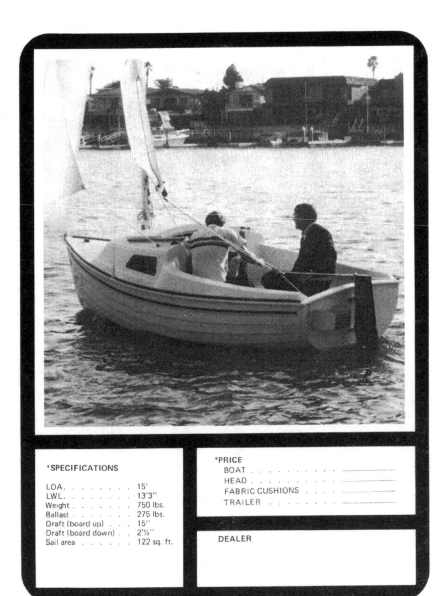

SPECIFICATIONS

LOA . . . . 15'
LWL . . . . 13'3"
Weight . . . . 750 lbs.
Ballast . . . . 275 lbs.
Draft (board up) . . . 15"
Draft (board down) . . 2'7½"
Sail area . . . . . . 122 sq. ft.

*PRICE
BOAT . . . .
HEAD . . . .
FABRIC CUSHIONS . . . .
TRAILER . . . .

DEALER

*Prices and specifications subject to change without notice

CHAPTER TWO

THE BOAT – LITTLE BREEZE

The beauty of the Montgomery 15 is its classic sloop design that includes a very roomy cuddy cabin incorporating an eight-foot V-berth. Lapstrakes formed in the fiberglass hull give the boat more stability and help to divert water, making for a drier sail. A partial keel with a small drop centerboard provides extra weight for stability while limiting draft restrictions, all of which make for a very finely crafted pocket cruiser.

The Montgomery 15 sloop is constructed from basically three prefabricated fiberglass forms, a deck, an interior liner, and a hull. It was very important that these were joined together properly. Marc designed a new reinforced hull-to-deck joint, which married these three forms together. This design was meant to withstand the kind of abuse and stresses that pound a boat in choppy seas. I think this included some extra Resin, glass and foam on the inside liner, seams, and joint. The hull-to-deck joint was then reinforced with the first one-piece teak toe rail, not the standard two-piece. The toe rail added strength and rigidity and gave me something to brace my toes against when trying to scramble around on a wet, slick, fiberglass deck.

Imbedded electrical wiring was added while laying up the gelcoat for the interior cabin, running lights, interior cabin light, and even a stereo. No electronics were offered on the M-15 at that time.

The aluminum spars and shrouds designed for the Montgomery 17 were cut down and adapted for the Montgomery 15. This included the first chain plates bolted to the side of the hull instead of the standard lighter weight deck hardware connection. Turnbuckles were also added to allow for extra fine tuning of the standing rigging.

I think Marc also supervised the fabricators as they laid up the fiberglass molds, making sure that a little extra Resin and glass were used.

The first bow pulpit was installed. One day completely by accident, Marc set down a Montgomery 17 bow pulpit onto the foredeck of my boat and noticed with a little bending it would fit nicely. The bow pulpit made it easier to handle sails at the bow.

Marc modified and installed a Montgomery 17 rudder instead of using the standard Montgomery 15 kick up rudder.

For additional safety, the first teak handrails were mounted on top of the cabin. This type handrails were standard on the M-17. During an installation on a 17, the end of a handrail had been damaged; Marc saw its usefulness, cut off the damaged end and installed this shorter version on my boat.

The cockpit lockers were expanded. The standard Montgomery 15 had small prefabricated bins molded into the cockpit. Marc cut the fiberglass interior of the port locker and fiberglassed in marine plywood, fore and aft under the cockpit, which added support for the cockpit, access to the motor mount nuts on the transom, and an enormous amount of storage space. Foam was added around the bin of the starboard locker, turning it into an icebox big enough for a six pack, a couple of sandwiches, and a bag of ice with room to spare. (This came in mighty handy for those hot summer months sailing around Huntington Harbor, Seal Beach, Long Beach, etc.) I know there were a few more changes; Marc was always contemplating ways to make this small boat *bullet proof*.

For about a year and a half I enjoyed sailing my *Little Breeze* throughout Huntington and Dana Point harbors and along the Seal Beach, Belmont Shores, and Long Beach waterfronts. Sailing had become my passion and every chance I got I would be out on the water, even by myself if I couldn't find someone to sail with me. The weather in Southern California is beautiful 360 days of the year, so you would find me out on my boat about every weekend. My *Little Breeze* was a great little sailboat that performed very well. I gradually built up enough confidence and experience to sail from Huntington Beach to Catalina Island on three separate occasions.

So back in the 5th Street Tavern, on that Friday night, there we were a couple of young guys wishing for and dreaming about sailing adventures, anything to get out of the humdrum life of working just to make enough money for rent and a night out on the weekend. We carried on until about one o'clock in the morning. A dozen napkins later, filled with notes and dreams, we called it a night and headed

CHAPTER TWO

home. Little did Marc realize that I *really* was considering making the trip! I wish I had saved some of those napkins.

CHAPTER THREE

ME – THE APPRENTICE

The winter of 1982 was a time in my life when I was yearning for change and adventure. I was the first born to Stuart and Janis Mann in Miami Beach, Florida, in October of 1959. Mom was a traditional housewife and mother. Dad was a new Navy doctor having recently completed medical school. When I was ten months old we moved to San Diego. Not soon after that relocation my dad left the military and we moved to Orange County where he began his private practice. I have lived most of my life in California ever since. Living in southern California near the ocean, especially in one of the more popular beach cities, one generally develops a love for the water and the outdoors.

As the years went by my folks had two more children, my sisters Stacy and Laurel. Sadly, around 1970, as I turned ten years old, my folks divorced and that was the end of what I thought was our happy little family. This was very hard on all of us. I struggled through junior high and as I entered high school my rebellious behavior became too much for my mom. She asked my dad to either take custody of me or find a place for me because she no longer wanted me living with her and my sisters. Since Dad had remarried to someone who

CHAPTER THREE

had two boys of her own, my moving in with him was not the best option. He made a great discovery though; a boarding school on Santa Catalina Island! Along with the regular high school curriculum, the school offered a broad spectrum of extracurricular activities such as kayaking, scuba diving, hiking, fishing, camping, and of course, sailing. I was sold on the school, enrolled as a sophomore in 1974 and graduated in 1977. This is where I met Marc, made many other friends, and had lots of other adventures, many of which I think helped prepare me for my solo voyage.

After high school graduation, I enrolled in Humboldt State University to major in oceanography. Discouraged by the huge class sizes and the fast pace of university life I only lasted there about one-and-a-half years. I moved to Port Angeles, Washington, with Pete McKnight, a childhood friend of mine, to work with him in his pole barn construction business. We never really had much work and I ended up going fishing for salmon and red snapper with his dad whenever the weather was good. I moved back in with Mom the summer of 1979, with the stipulation that I attend junior college and that I pay rent. I spent a year at Orange Coast College, Costa Mesa, California, and graduated in June 1980 with an Associate of Arts degree in Marine Technology. During that year I was working part time at Marine Biological Consultants (MBC) in Costa Mesa in the same industrial area as Montgomery Marine Products.

MBC produced environmental impact reports for business and construction projects along the southern California coastline. The 1980s were the start of a lot of this type of reporting. Marc and I were living and working close to each other and would spend many weekends sailing on his ketch. Eventually we became roommates.

After graduating from Orange Coast College, I continued working at MBC, but with business slowing I was laid off fourteen months later. By this time I had bought my boat. I named her *Little Breeze*, not just because she would sail great in a little breeze, but also after the Lynyrd Skynyrd song "The Breeze." (Marc had named his Montgomery 17 *FreeBird* after another Skynyrd song.)

I soon got a job working for Southern California Soils and Testing (SCST) as a grading inspector. My job description included going to job sites where they were grading and compacting building pads and trenches. It was my job to test for compaction. If the ground didn't meet the specs I would tell the foreman to continue compacting the soil until it met specifications. This was a great job because I was outside all day traveling from one job site to another. The downside was dealing with the contractors on the site who would become angry when I informed them the ground was too wet or too dry or not compact enough. They could not get signed off on the job until I had approved and written up my report. Although this was a fun job, it had no future. It was during this time that I started daydreaming at work and brought in *Cruising World* sailing magazines to read in my truck while waiting for contractors to call me over to test sites.

I began immersing myself in nautical adventure and training books. Marc had been giving me books about sailing adventures to read like:

Tinkerbelle by Robert Manry

Alone Against the Atlantic by Gerry Spiess

CHAPTER THREE

After 50,000 Miles by Hal Roth

Self-Steering by John Letcher

And of course the old classic,
The Dove by Robin Graham.

My dreaming, contemplating, sailing, and reading were all converging and in the winter of 1982, while still working as a grading inspector, I decided to plan to sail solo to Hawaii.

That first eventful night at the 5th Street Tavern I asked Marc for his advice and suggestions. Truthfully, all the planning and preparations were as exciting as the trip itself.

Just before starting to transform the *Little Breeze* into an open ocean cruiser I made my first solo sail out to Catalina. I left on a Saturday, spent the night at Goat Harbor and sailed back on Sunday. It was a pleasant trip. I felt comfortable alone, but could see that I needed to make some changes to my boat. It was around the beginning of April 1982 when I brought the boat to Marc's sister house on Sandpiper Avenue, Huntington Beach, to work under his supervision. Marc was a boat builder I was not. You might say that I was his apprentice. I learned a lot about fabrication, fiberglass, and general seamanship skills from Marc during the days and weeks to follow, not to mention he had all the tools that I needed. I probably couldn't have made the trip if I had to buy all the tools he let me use.

CHAPTER FOUR

Breaking the News to Family and Friends

I worked bit by bit and piece by piece every evening after work and on weekends. There were so many little details to consider, not only modifications to the boat, but I had to teach myself celestial navigation (at least how to shoot sun lines), and obtain all the supplies, provisions, and equipment. I used inventory lists found in the appendices in the books *Tinkerbelle* and *Alone Against the Atlantic* as blueprints for single-handed sailing life, to make hard choices on equipment and provisions, and how I would pack and prepare for the voyage.

At the end of April I decided to tell my family and friends of my plans to sail alone to Hawaii. Needless to say this did not go over well with my parents. Ever since their split-up, they lived in close proximity to each other, Mom lived in Fountain Valley and Dad in Huntington Beach. I lived between Mom's and Marc's house during these preliminary days. Dad being a doctor mainly worried about my physical and mental well-being. Mom feared for my life and just knew that she would never see "her boy" again.

One night Dad and his wife Frances invited me out to

eat. I thought this would be as good a time as any to let them know of my plans. We had just ordered dinner when I said, "Dad I am preparing to sail my boat to Hawaii this summer." I was watching for my dad's response, but he did not grasp what I had just said and kept looking at the dessert menu. Frances, on the other hand, immediately said, "You are going to die! Stuart, did you hear him? Tell him!" My dad was not what you might call an outdoors type person, but he finally got the idea and thinking like a physician he looked at me and asked, "Have you ever heard of sensory deprivation?" I told him I knew what that meant and assured him that I was taking every possible precaution. Frances asked, "Michael, answer me one question. Have you ever spent twenty-four hours completely alone?" I had to admit, "No I haven't," and with that she threw up her hands as if to say, "Need I say more?" It was a quiet dinner after that. I tried to share some of the accounts I had been reading, stories of men who had sailed in smaller boats, farther distances and in rougher waters, but Dad and Frances would have none of it. For weeks they would try to talk me out of going.

    As my departure drew near and they could see that I was still serious about the trip, they became a little more helpful. They let me tie my boat up at the dock behind their house in Huntington Harbor, most likely so that they could keep an eye on me as I made my final preparations. Dad came down to the boat one day to examine my first aid kit. He gave me some antibiotics and something for pain. Francis made up a little goodie bag of nuts, M&Ms, raisins, assorted candies, some socks, sweat shirts and pants.

    I told Mom of my sailing plans late one evening after

she had come from her customary Friday night bridge game. We were sitting in the kitchen when I said, "Mom, I am planning on sailing my boat to Hawaii this summer." She replied, "That's nice dear, who is going with you?" I told her that my boat was a little small so my plan was to go by myself. I could see the tears welling up in her eyes and then she could not hold them back any longer and tears started streaming down her cheeks.

Another night, with only a couple of weeks to go until my departure, I was studying celestial navigation in the kitchen and Mom kept interrupting me. I turned to her and loudly said, "*Mom, leave me alone!* I have to learn this or it could cost me my life!" Well that did it; she left the room really crying!

From that day on whenever Mom came home from work or playing bridge and saw me sitting at the table studying, she would ask if I was still going. When I would say yes, she would leave the room sobbing. As the actual departure date drew near she had convinced herself that the only way that she could endure my absence was if she bought me a VHF radio, in the hopes of me getting a message back that I was alright. My boat wasn't very high tech and I couldn't afford the first generation of solar panels or bulky wind generators to keep my 12-volt car batteries charged. I told her that chances were slim that I would really encounter other boats to talk to, but I humored her and bought a handheld VHF radio for about two hundred eighty dollars, a lot of money back then. I never did get that message back along the way, but the radio did come in handy as we'll see later.

CHAPTER FIVE

Practice and Preparations

Once preparations began in earnest, I was completely focused, even obsessed with working on the boat. Some nights Marc and I would take a break while his sister Laura made us dinner. Later we would head over to 5th Street Tavern and pick up where we had left off with dreaming and planning the next great sailing adventure, except now we were actually working toward our goals, my trip to Hawaii on my M-15 *Little Breeze* and Marc's trip around the world on his M-17 *Freebird*.

When April rolled into May, it seemed that time was running short. June is generally the best time of year to sail to Hawaii from Southern California. I would get to Marc's house in the evening after working eight to ten hours at SCST only to work another three to four hours there, most of the time by drop light or flashlight as we worked long into the night. My to-do list seemed to keep growing.

A couple of other gentlemen in my sphere of influence were Jerry Montgomery and Stan Susman. Jerry was the owner and operator of Montgomery Marine Products, a small boat manufacturer in Costa Mesa, California. Jerry encouraged me and had a lot of good ideas. He said that he

CHAPTER FIVE

would ship my boat home if I would come right back from Hawaii. He liked the idea of me sailing to Hawaii in one of his boats—what great publicity if I made it.

Stan was the manager of the Captain's Locker, a marine hardware store in Newport Beach, California. He was a friend of both Jerry and Marc and a heck of a nice guy. Stan took a keen interest and was always asking if I had what he considered the basics in safety equipment. He took my trip quite seriously and wouldn't let me buy poor quality equipment. I ended up spending about two hundred dollars a week at the Captain's Locker. I never had a budget; I bought what I thought I needed with the money I had saved.

As the departure day approached, Stan went over my equipment list and loaned (gave) me items that I would likely overlook because I had just about run out of money. I think I left California with barely two hundred dollars cash. I bought a portable strobe light, a simple and effective aid that I could lash in the rigging or hoist to the top of my mast to be more visible at night to larger vessels. He gave me a simple little radar reflector that I could hoist or lash in the rigging where it would not interfere with the sails. Stan also gave me a small pop rivet set because he said that in a pinch I could drill and pop rivet hardware in place quicker than tapping and screwing. Finally, I think it was Stan who thought of and gave me a portable cassette recorder. Without this contribution I would not have the tape recorded record of my journey.

My preparations also included reading numerous magazines and books and talking with other sailors on what I might expect in the way of weather and seas on the way

PRACTICE AND PREPARATIONS

to Hawaii. People who had sailed to Hawaii said that due to the trade winds, it was about the easiest downwind trip to make. My plan to sail a fifteen-foot boat alone brought varied comments from "Good luck" to "You're crazy!" My friend's father, Harry Moloshco, who is the owner of the sailboat *Drifter* and a former winner of the renowned Transpac yacht race (the race from Los Angeles to Hawaii) asked—jokingly I think—if he could take insurance out on me through Lloyd's of London.

Time was passing quickly and of course the cost of the trip had exceeded my savings. The goal was to leave the first of June but I needed more time to earn much needed funds, prepare my boat and learn celestial navigation.

I studied how to complete a sun line using the book *Practical Navigation* by Neil Walker. Every chance I could get, late in the afternoon, I would drive to the beach to practice taking sun sights with a sextant. Celestial navigation, also known as astronavigation, is a position fixing technique that has evolved over several hundred years to help sailors cross oceans. That was what I intended to do. Celestial navigation is used to locate one's position on the globe through the use of angular measurements "sights" between the sun, moon or stars and the visible horizon, time and mathematical tables. For the unobstructed horizon needed to take a sun sight, I would drive to the parking lot at the bluffs above the beach at the end of Newfoundland Avenue and the Pacific Coast Highway. From there I could look to the southwest over a clear view of the Pacific Ocean to the horizon.

A sextant is used to measure the angle of the celestial body above the visible horizon. With the precise time of the sight by chronometer, one can extrapolate from the tables to produce a "line of sight" to plot on a chart. The sextant, a plastic Davis Mark 15, was my first big purchase of one hundred twenty five dollars. I used a twenty dollar Casio Chronometer I bought at Kmart for my time piece. I had to practice using a sextant to bring the sun down and swing its lower limb on the horizon. I would record the time and the height of the sight then head home to work out the calculations. I needed a Nautical Almanac and the sight reduction tables H.O. 249 to "reduce" the sights. It takes about thirty minutes for a novice to complete the calculation and plot the results on a plotting sheet or chart.

I was pleased whenever my sun lines would fall over (or near) where I had parked to take the sight. I took the sights in about the same place at the same time each day. This was not the same as advancing lines from sights throughout the day to actually produce a "fix". I really didn't have the time to get out on the water all day for that kind of practice so I would just have to believe that I could get by with knowing the mechanics of the procedure and do my best during the voyage.

My day usually went as follows: I worked all day at SCST then went to Marc's, worked several additional hours on the boat, then head home to study navigation and do more research before I could drag myself to bed. My sleep was restless. I was starting to dream about what the trip would be like and what I would go through. Later I would recall that I had lived out the entire trip in my dreams before I even got started.

I purchased a pair of twin headsails from Marc. These

would be handy for what I was hoping would be mostly a downwind run to Hawaii, although I would have to travel far enough west and offshore to hit the "trade winds" which generally blew from east to the west. (Named from their ability to quickly propel trading ships across the ocean, the trade winds between about 30 degrees latitude and the equator are steady and typical speeds range between 12-18 knots.) As a precaution, I also purchased a 170% Genoa sail (just in case of light airs). I had both sails cut down at McKibbin Sails to fit my boat's profile.

Whisker poles would be needed to hold out the clew of the twin jibs so that when sailing downwind the sails could fill more effectively. I thought it would be a great idea to mount them on deck to make them easily accessible. Marc showed me how to drill and tap holes on the forward edge of the mast to mount the track needed for the sliding padeye. The padeye was used to connect 2 seven-foot whisker poles and then two additional padeyes were mounted on deck for the lower end of the poles. The whisker poles, permanently stored here, forward of the mast, made an upside down "^" shape. I found that this was a place I could retreat to in turbulent weather. The poles were strong enough that I could hold on and find refuge between them while working with the sails.

Preparations continue—Next I replaced the smaller stock cleats with larger cleats. Marc had shown me the technique of "backing up" cleats and blocks attached to the deck by bolting aluminum or wood backing plates underneath each cleat to strengthen it. This would minimize the chance that the cleat would pull out of the deck under heavy strain. All

CHAPTER FIVE

deck hardware was bound to take a heavy strain; inserting a piece of wood or metal plates on the underside of the deck would help to spread the load.

Thicker teak cabin drop boards were installed. I installed a small four-inch diameter clear plastic porthole in the top of the third drop board, so that I could at least look aft into the cockpit from inside the cabin. The bottom board was permanently caulked and bolted in place to keep water from making its way into the cabin should the cockpit be flooded. The old drop boards were cut and fitted to make segregations and stiffeners for the cabin lockers under the V-berth. Two small gear hammocks were hung in the cabin beneath the cabin portholes to store loose gear.

I relocated the mainsheet cleat (originally below the companionway) from the thwart, to the bottom of the cockpit sole. The thwart was 13/16 inch thick teak, which is pretty strong, but the sheet's location interfered with access to the cabin. Mounting it to the cockpit sole allowed me easier access while also spreading out the loads on the mainsheet.

In May, Marc decided that he would bring his *Freebird* to Laura's house to make the modifications he wanted for his big voyage. Now there were two boats on trailers parked on the front lawn and we looked like a regular boatyard. The city gave notice to Laura that the boats were not to be stored on the front lawn.

Little Breeze had the approved running lights for her size and class mounted on deck, but since I would be in seas and swells as high as twenty feet I needed to mount a mast head tri-color light for greater visibility.

I mounted a Forespar Mini-Galley gimbaled stove on

PRACTICE AND PREPARATIONS

the fixed lower drop board just inside the cabin. The stove used small propane cartridges and had a cage to hold one small aluminum pot. The unit is designed to remain upright even as the boat rolls and pitches in the seas.

I started thinking about *Little Breeze's* survivability, about taking seas over the stern from a rogue wave or—heaven forbid—being turned over. I decided to fill all my empty spars with two-part expansion foam for buoyancy. If the boat did layover or turn over, a mast full of foam would at least help to start the righting process. Working with two-part foam is easy, but tricky. It is hard to calculate the amount to mix to fill a specific volume of empty space. After mixing equal amounts of foam and catalyst in a bucket and stirring well, the foam would go off like a Fourth of July fireworks snake and start hardening and expanding. I stood on a six-foot backyard brick wall so I could quickly pour the mixture down my hollow nineteen-foot aluminum mast while elevating one end. The expanding foam would start spilling out both ends of the mast with little I could do to contain the foam. No problem, after the foam hardened and cooled I gathered all the spillage for the trash. I also filled the boom and my two whisker poles. I tested the new buoyancy of my mast, boom, and whisker poles by throwing them into a neighbor's swimming pool. Success—they all stayed afloat.

Another concern was that of a large wave rolling over the gunwales and filling up the open seven-foot cockpit with seawater, and what the weight of that water might do to the boat's buoyancy. I decided to drill and install 3 three-quarter inch drain plugs at the rear of the cockpit. These were positioned one on each side and one in dead center of the footwell exiting through the transom to the sea in the hopes of quickly draining sea water from the cockpit. Although I needed the drainage ability, I had drilled my first holes into the boat's hull. My new skills of mounting through-hull fittings would be tested because I had to shimmy from inside the cabin, under the cockpit sole, to the transom to reach the fittings. If there were any leaks, I would not be able to get to these to tighten them up again while at sea.

To help reduce the volume of cockpit space, which I really didn't need for myself, I cut out a large piece of Styrofoam and lashed it to the rear of the cockpit. This came in handy the couple of times I slipped and fell on the wet decks. Instead of injuring myself by falling on the hard fiberglass I fell back on the soft Styrofoam which prevented serious injury.

Many of these additions helped to drain and reduce the collection of water above decks, but what if water made it into the cabin? I couldn't imagine just bailing with a bucket so I installed a manual "Whale Gusher" bilge pump in the cabin footwell. These pumps could really move large volumes of water in a hurry. The suction hose end was long enough to reach anywhere in the cabin. The discharge hose end was run aft and went through another through-hull fitting in the transom. Another hole in the hull!

As the work continued on *Little Breeze* at Marc's house, there were other projects going on at my mom's house, where I was living at the time. I had filled up 20 one-liter plastic Seven Up, Coke, and Pepsi bottles with water and stacked them in the corner of the backyard to see if any leaked. These were going to be my fresh water containers.

PRACTICE AND PREPARATIONS

Before stacking them I smashed, kicked, and tossed them to the ground to learn that, in fact, a plaster liter bottle is virtually indestructible. Later after picking the best bottles, I rinsed and filled them again with fresh water and proceeded to seal the caps by dipping them into a small pot of melted paraffin wax. I also tested 18 one-gallon Clorox bottles and a five-gallon jug Marc had given me. I ended up with about thirty-four gallons of water.

I was a regular pack rat collecting waterproof containers to protect stores and equipment. Gerry Spiess, who sailed *Yankee Girl* across the Atlantic in 1979, had used one-gallon, wide mouth, plastic jugs, like those that large condiments come in for school commissaries. I checked with Marina High and Huntington Beach High only to find out that they did not obtain their condiments in this type container. I remembered the Ichthyoplankton specimen jugs used by my former employer, MBC. They were delighted to give me the jugs I needed.

One possible construction flaw with the Montgomery 15, for the ocean crossing I was planning, was an unsupported mast. The mast was just stepped or mounted on top of the fiberglass cabin without a compression post affixed beneath that would support the downward forces of the mast and transfer this force to the more solid keel. The Montgomery 15 was not originally built to withstand possible gale force winds. A compression post would have passed right through the center of the V-berth in the cabin and interfere with the living space. I asked my brother-in-law, a welder, to weld the mast step to a 10 x 12 x 3/8-inch thick stainless steel plate that he had molded to the contour of the cabin top. He

CHAPTER FIVE

also fabricated the backup plate for inside the cabin. I could now sandwich the cabin top between these solid plates and this in turn would now distribute the compression loads. Given these modifications, I never worried about the mast breaking through the cabin above and crushing me while I was sleeping.

Two battery boxes were installed in the space under the forward, center, V-berth. I needed power to operate my running lights and cabin light. I carried two 12-volt car batteries which actually lasted for a very long time.

One dilemma that came up in my readings, especially in small boats, was to have a way to keep from being tossed about the cabin in violent seas. My solution was to cut in two an old diving weight belt strap and fasten the belt pieces to the seat inside the cabin. Should I find myself bouncing around in the cabin I intended to strap myself down.

I purchased a very nice Danforth bulkhead mounted compass. This instrument was my most important piece of equipment. Without a dependable compass I would be lost. After installing the compass on the cabin face, to the left of the companionway, I took the boat to Newport Harbor where I hired a compass surveyor to help me swing my compass and prepare a deviation correction card. The surveyor remarked that this was the smallest boat he'd ever swung a compass for.

The second most important piece of equipment was the VDO sumlog or knot log/meter. The sumlog would tell me the speed of the boat to help me fine tune the sails and keep the accurate total of miles traveled through the water. To plot my position in open-ocean by "dead reckoning" or

"DR" I would need to know my direction (by compass) and speed and distance (by sumlog) to estimate my position during periods where celestial navigation was not possible. As a part of navigation, direction as well as speed and distance, are needed to plot positions. The sumlog did not use electricity but a mechanical cable that worked like a bicycle odometer cable. To mount the sumlog propeller, I had to drill a quarter-inch hole in the bottom of the hull, about a foot to the left of the keel. As with all my through-hull fittings, I fashioned a very sturdy backup block of teak so I could really caulk and cinch down on the retaining nut. The cable snaked from under the cockpit sole to the back of the sumlog mileage/speed display which was mounted on the cabin to the right of the companionway. As the boat moved through the water the impeller would spin, turning the inner cable, this in turn rotated the knot meter, so the mileage meter would display the miles traveled. It had both a total miles display and a display that could be reset to zero by pushing a button. This allowed me to keep track of my daily runs. Without this mileage information I would never know how far I had traveled.

CHAPTER SIX

Putting It All Together

May 21 – I gave my two week notice to Southern California Soils and Testing. The vice president of the company thought it was a worthwhile adventure and wished me luck.

Near the end of May all the major modifications and additions had been made. Now it was time for a test run. I planned a trip from Long Beach, around the backside of Catalina Island, and down to Dana Point where Marc would meet me with my car and trailer. Marc drove me down to the Long Beach Harbor boat ramp at Golden Shores where I launched and headed out. The new sails, rigging, and instruments would be put to the test. All went well, except that the winds in southern California are mostly light and variable, so I ended up motoring for long periods when there was no wind at all. In addition, my sights were not as easy to obtain and plot at sea as they were while standing on stable ground. Thirty-six hours later after nonstop sailing I arrived at the Dana Point Harbor launch ramp where I immediately fell asleep! As I was waiting for Marc to pick me up, a harbor patrol officer stopped and gave me a ticket for not having my registration for the boat. I had applied for new tags from the Department of Motor Vehicles weeks earlier. I told the

CHAPTER SIX

harbor patrol officer that I was still waiting for my tags, but he'd probably heard that before. I think it was a fifty dollar fine—fifty dollars I could hardly spare at the time.

Another important skill I had been mastering, even before planning a trip to Hawaii, was what is referred to as "sheet-to-tiller" self-steering. If you are sailing alone there is no way to sit at the tiller twenty-four hours a day. You have to eat and sleep and keep the boat moving at all times. A sailboat has natural steering ability if you can manage to set the tiller at just the correct angle to offset the forces of the wind. *Little Breeze's* steering ability was accomplished using a variety of bungee cords, block and tackle fastened to the tiller, through a block on the gunwale and then tied either to the mainsheet or jib sheet. I used John Letcher's book, *Self-Steering for Small Sailing Craft*, to come up with the ideas and techniques. Sheet-to-tiller steering capitalizes on the simple principle that the same forces that cause a sailboat to go off course, are used to steer in a counteracting direction to keep it on course. Most sailboats are designed so that the helm is balanced in light air, but weather helm increases as the angle of heel increases due to the force of the wind on the sails. This causes most boats to round up into the wind so the rudder is used to keep the boat on course. When properly adjusted, the same force on the sails that cause this rounding up can be transmitted directly through a line and blocks to the tiller, to keep the boat on its desired course.

Some techniques worked, some didn't, and some just needed to be modified for *Little Breeze* and circumstances. In the end, I would only be physically sailing her when the need arose; mostly I would just tend to the self-steering gear.

PUTTING IT ALL TOGETHER

May 28 and 29 – After sailing around Catalina I brought *Little Breeze* to Montgomery's shop for some last minute work which included a new coat of bottom paint donated by Jerry.

May 30 – I picked the boat up from Montgomery Marine and then later met up with Whitney (another friend from Catalina Island School) and Jack (a co-worker from SCST) at the Huntington Harbor boat ramp. We all piled into *Little Breeze* and motored out through the Huntington Harbor and into Long Beach Harbor. These were some pretty big guys I had with me so I was able to get a feel for the boat with a little weight in her, as well as have a good time on the water. We stopped in a calm spot to heel the boat over as far as we could. The three of us hung onto the mast and shifted our weight to one side, almost putting the gunwale in the water, before letting her go. We fell into the water and watched the boat spring straight up and right herself. We swam around a bit before climbing back in to sail for home. At the end of the day, we said our good-byes. Whitney gave me some music he had recorded on cassettes and Jack gave me his Kodak Instamatic camera. Unfortunately, the camera and pictures would later be stolen from my boat.

June 2 – All looks ready. I know I could use more time, but truly all I need is the remainder of my supplies and some spare bottom paint, before I can at last begin loading the boat. I will sail out of Huntington Harbor and leave from the Long Beach area. I plan to anchor or moor at Catalina Harbor for one last night of full slumber and then it will be out to sea for who knows what!

I have asked myself why I am doing this and my first

CHAPTER SIX

sarcastic answer is "Why not?" For the past several months my life has had purpose. I have had more fun and adventures planning and preparing for this trip than I have had in a long time. I have met a lot of neat people, some who encouraged me and some who just told me I was insane. As far as I could tell my planning and working for this goal takes nothing away from my future, but will only add experience and wisdom. Maybe I will truly see my worth and rationally plan for the long haul—for the rest of my days. Soon it will be up to me and me alone.

Good luck and happy sailing. May my boat be willing and a good breeze at my back. (I haven't even left yet and I am already talking to myself!)

My California coast days were numbered now. With my last paycheck from work, I planned to go on a wild pre-voyage shopping spree.

The week before I set sail, Dad invited me to meet him at the Long Beach Yacht Club where he was a member, for sort of a going away dinner. I wondered if he was still opposed to my sailing venture. I really couldn't imagine what Dad would say at dinner. I needed his moral support. What I hoped for was that he would be optimistic and positive with me.

It has been ten years since my parents divorced and we all pretty much had taken our own paths in life to pursue our own interests and we were not a close family. Regarding my decision to sail to Hawaii, I was surprised that anyone truly cared. I wasn't making the trip to get attention. I was on my own quest and my own journey in life.

Well, Dad wanted one more stab at changing my mind. He said it wouldn't be fair to put the family through the waiting, wondering and anxiety of what might happen. A few of Dad's friends stopped by our table to meet me. Quickly the conversation turned to how unpredictable the weather could be on the Hawaii transit and how some guys in well-equipped boats have trouble with the trip. Guess it will be up to me to change Dad's opinion of my abilities and diminish the fears he may have of what he thought was my wild impulsiveness.

June 4 – This was my last day at work. Kay, the secretary, baked me a cake and had planned a surprise Bon Voyage party. The hour party was spent eating cake and telling tales of my upcoming sailing adventure. My six months with SCST over, I headed for my car wondering if I would ever see any of these people again. I really started to feel the impact of what I was about to do. What felt like a rush of electricity flowed through my body and I was flying on a cloud.

My mom's poor condo was now a marine hardware store with piles of sails, a rubber raft, tools, stove, charts, foul weather gear, etc. all over the living room. Everything was laid out for inventory.

One final investment was the food. I had been watching the papers and noting the sales up until this point. My main meals would be basically Dinty Moore beef stew, chili, and soups. They were in the normal twelve-ounce size cans. The assorted canned fruit and vegetables would be in smaller six-ounce sizes. Jack and I must have been a comical sight as we filled up three shopping carts with groceries. At home, we pulled the paper labels off and used a black grease pencil to put the content names back on the cans. Jack pulled a fast one on me and wrote little messages on some of the cans

CHAPTER SIX

instead of the name, like a "?" or "Guess what this is?"

After packaging and sealing up my provisions, it was time to start moving all my equipment and supplies to the *Little Breeze* docked behind my father's house. All my gear, when laid out, covered the twelve-by-forty-foot dock. All this, plus me, was supposed to fit in my little boat. I could only estimate that all this stuff, including food and water, must have weighed 700 pounds while my boat alone weighed 950 pounds.

I tried to pack in order of necessity, last things first, first things last. I prepared an inventory list by location on the boat so I could remember where I packed each item. (See appendices.)

Time was passing quickly so I started saying my good-byes. Of course Mom would just cry when she saw me. I was invited out by friends to a couple of going away parties. Dad invited me out to dinner a few nights before I sailed. Dad, Frances, her son Marshal, his friend Jimmy, and I met at the El Torito for some excellent Mexican food. Frances brought up the fact that there had been a tragic accident at sea during a sailboat race near England. A freak storm swept down over the racers and many boats and several lives were lost. I guess this was their last attempt to get me to reconsider my plans.

(Above) Ready for her bottom coat at Montgomery's shop
(Opposite) Installing the Styrofoam block, Refashioning the drop boards, Little Breeze sitting on Laura's front lawn

CHAPTER SEVEN

LET THE VOYAGE BEGIN

Thursday
June 10, 1982

LOG

0039
(Lying alongside Dad's dock
behind his home in Huntington Harbor.)
Making ready for departure in the morning.
Expecting light and variable winds
through Friday night, cloudy Friday and Saturday.
Weather to start clearing Saturday afternoon.
Local winds out of west Friday.
Trade winds 200 miles to the south;
winds 15 knots out of the east.
Chance of tropical storms zero percent
(or so I thought just prior to sailing).
Weak high pressure system
in area through weekend.
Good luck to me!

CHAPTER SEVEN

JOURNAL

Had a quiet dinner at the house with Dad and Frances. I grilled steak and potatoes on the patio barbeque. I had spent the last three nights sleeping on the boat getting acclimated to my living space following each full day of packing.

On my last evening, Dad came down to the boat and sat with me in the cockpit. As the sun was setting and the stars began coming out Dad and I sat quietly. This was an awkward moment—father and son wondering if we would ever see each other again. Dad expressed his concern, but wished me well and asked that I return as soon as possible. It was a bittersweet moment. Had my family shown this much love and concern for each other in the past, as they were for me right now, maybe I would not be sitting here preparing to sail off by myself to Hawaii on a fifteen-foot boat!

As I sit in my boat and write this entry by flashlight, so as to conserve on 12-volt battery power, I am going over and over in my head everything that has led up to this trip. My reasons for going are numerous and will take a great deal of time to fully explain. To all those people that have stared at me in disbelief when I told them about sailing a fifteen-foot sail boat to Hawaii, I say that I am ready to set out and accomplish my dream; what dreams have you pursued with a passion? Marc Hightower is a good friend to whom I owe much. He is the one that taught me to sail, taught me the excitement and exhilaration of making a boat glide across the water with only the wind in a sail. It was by his guidance that I was able to set my goal into motion and on into this present reality. I am dedicating this trip to him and to his future adventures.

Thinking back now to that night sitting in the 5th Street Tavern going over my initial plans, lists of equipment, and modifications needed to the boat, it is hard to believe that when I untie the lines and start down the channel in the morning I am actually going to try and sail to Hawaii! Together we planned and dreamed while drinking some beer and shooting pool. I really didn't have big dreams before I met Marc, but here was a person who wasn't satisfied with the status quo. Marc's piercing blue eyes were always gazing out over the horizon. After sailing with Marc over the years I too got the vision. I think the need to break out and away from a monotonous suburban life might be a common trait among young men from fractured families and whose foundation and security have been shaken. Many of those kids may become self-absorbed and antisocial and end up seeking pleasure with sex, drugs, and rock-n-roll—or sailing to Hawaii in a fifteen-foot boat.

I wish to take this time to thank Stan Susman and Jerry Montgomery; this trip would not have been possible without their contributions, advice, and materials. I really have to get some sleep now.

Tomorrow the tides of a young man's dream will transport him into a great and awe inspiring adventure.

Friday
June 11 – Day 1

LOG
1900
VDO Sum Log

CHAPTER SEVEN

Initially reads – 28.5 miles
Arrive Cabrillo Beach Anchorage – 39.6 miles
Wind and swell coming from the southwest
made it hard to make it offshore today.
Decided to hold up and rearrange gear
at Cabrillo Beach. Will leave with first wind
in the morning and will make for the West End
of Catalina Island tomorrow.
Took a sight en route and was within
three miles of Dead Reckoning position (DR).
Watch error 18 seconds fast.

JOURNAL

I said good-bye to Dad and Frances as they left for work this morning and a short time later got a phone call from Jack wishing me luck. It was hard to imagine what everyone felt as I prepared to depart. All the good-byes were short and sweet. Who knows, they all must have had their own fears and misgivings.

I decided to treat myself to one last home cooked breakfast of bacon, eggs, and toast. I sat on the patio watching my *Little Breeze* lazily lying there tied to the dock. I was just about to cast off and head out on a voyage that really was inconceivable even for the most seasoned sailor when I thought to myself, "Here I am a novice sailor, about to tackle the Pacific Ocean in a fifteen-foot sailboat." I started to think of Gerry Spiess and his trips on the ten-foot *Yankee Girl*. At least I had almost two years of experience sailing my boat all around Southern California, but Spiess designed, built, and sailed off in his boat without much testing in ocean waters. Plus I had a full five more feet than *Yankee Girl*. I just knew in my heart that *Little Breeze* was sea worthy! My hope was that I was just as sea worthy as *Little Breeze*.

With one last look over the boat I was satisfied that all my gear was secured and it was time to go! This was an emotional moment as I cast off the mooring lines myself, since no one was there to help me, and drifted off the dock. There was no big fanfare; Marc had gone hiking and only a handful of people knew of my plans.

I pulled the starting cord on my three-and-one-half horse power British Seagull outboard and the motor coughed to life. I wanted to sail out of the harbor, but harbor regulations did not permit sailing through Seal Beach Naval Weapons Station, which is situated at the head waters of Huntington Harbor. Sailors are required to transit the station under power. I had tried sailing once before only to have the Harbor Patrol chase me down. I wanted to rebel and sail through the Naval Station, but it was already eleven o'clock in the morning and I didn't want any further delay.

As I motored through the harbor I passed many boats and I waved and smiled. Little did the people know that I was headed for Hawaii in my little boat. Even in the protected waters of Huntington Harbor, I could tell that *Little Breeze* was riding a little low in the water, especially at the bow, but she felt stable.

Around 12:30 p.m. I had made it to the end of the breakwater and out into the open sea only to find almost no wind. The boat was a little hard to handle in these light airs so I decided to make for San Pedro. I would hold up there

CHAPTER SEVEN

for the night to have a better jumping off angle for clearing Catalina Island the next day. I ran the gas out of the fuel line so that the fuel wouldn't solidify and clog up the fuel line and carburetor. Since the motor would be exposed to every wave that came up to the stern and over the transom motor mount, I sealed my precious little outboard in three layers of sturdy garbage bags and secured it with duct tape. Then I added extra rope lashings to the port stern cleat because this is where it would be stored for the rest of the voyage. I couldn't afford to ship the motor ahead so it would sit on my transom. Carrying a large amount of gasoline on *Little Breeze* was out of the question for many reasons.

Later that night—I am a little disappointed with myself for not overcoming my difficulty in heading offshore. Wind and swell both coming from southwest. With the boat being a little heavy at the bow I just couldn't keep up any momentum against the swell. By making the stop in San Pedro, I at least got a chance to try and reorganize everything. The boat is packed chuck-a-block full; should have taken a few pictures of the stowage inside the cabin, but *Little Breeze* is performing well under the burden.

VDO seems to be accurate; I wish I had adjusted the rig so the forestay was a little tighter, but I think it will be alright.

My first operational challenge came as I accidentally dropped the pin for the anchor chain shackle as I was making ready to drop the anchor. I lost the pin under a pile of gear which was also stowed in the anchor chain locker. Simultaneously, I had the anchor rode flaked out in the cockpit sole, found the shackle pin, properly shackled the rode to the anchor, dropped the anchor over the side, and had it fetched up nice and tight, all while sailing single-handed in dim light as the sun was setting. These are the sort of reflex skills a single-handed sailor must master.

Tomorrow should be a real good day. I feel bad that everyone is worrying about me when I am snug and cozy at anchor in San Pedro. Ah well, they will have to get used to it.

I think I may have packed too many clothes. There isn't a lot of room for me to stretch out fully in the cabin. My living space is much like being in a small camping tent. There is only one little area where I can sit up (not quite straight up) and I have just enough room to lie down with about two feet between me and the companionway opening.

CHAPTER EIGHT

Disappointing first days

Saturday
June 12 – Day 2

LOG
0849
San Pedro Entrance
Variable nonexistent course,
1.6 nautical miles traveled.
A little breeze in the morning,
but it died when I got to harbor entrance.
1315
Approximately 3.5 miles SW of Point Fermin.
Course (Cse) – 27° true
2 knots, 3.4 nautical miles traveled.
Cloudy with some fog.
1752
33°32'N
118°29'W
6.0 nautical miles traveled.
Wind picking up to 15 knots.
15.2 nautical miles daily run
26.3 total nautical miles traveled

CHAPTER EIGHT

JOURNAL

The West End of Catalina is in sight. I just finished a grand dinner of Dinty Moore beef stew which included some dried minced onions and zucchini in my first meal at sea in my little Forespar Mini-Galley butane stove. The gimbaled stove, mounted just inside the cabin on the drop board, is free to tilt and remain in an upright position even as the boat rolls and pitches in these small seas. The small blue metal butane cartridge just screws into the bottom of the burner. I turn the valve to release the gas, light a match, set the tin pot filled with cold Dinty Moore in the keeper ring over the flame and a hot meal is ready in no time. Cooking meals myself will be something I have to do every day. I have to eat to keep up my strength. Now I have to clean up the mess. Cleaning up is actually more trouble than cooking. I have to reach out of the cabin and over the side to get a small amount of seawater in my little bucket and then with a Brillo pad, work at scraping out the burnt Dinty Moore in the bottom of my little tin one-quart pot.

Another two hours of daylight remain. I just hope the wind keeps up a little after dark so I can clear the West End. If I can clear this first big obstacle then I can sort of drift away from the rocky point of Catalina and towards the distant San Clemente Island while I try and lie down to get a couple hours of sleep.

Well, it's ten thirty at night and it doesn't look like I'll be rounding the West End tonight. Wind is twenty knots from the west. I have the storm jib up and both reefs in main. Six-foot swell with chop. I see the West End light and all I have to do is make enough leeway to clear the point. It is rock and roll out here. There are hundreds of little pinpoints of light in an otherwise black night. The lights of San Pedro are plain to see behind me in the distance. Tomorrow I have to get better organized. My cramped quarters are in a shambles and if this is just a taste of what is to come, I will be real miserable if it starts to rain. I am going to try and get some sleep. I am exhausted.

TAPE

"Sitting off the breakwater at San Pedro waiting for some wind. Didn't quite make it to the island yesterday. Fought head-on swells and winds the whole way and decided to spend the night at Cabrillo to get things rearranged. I had some breeze in the morning that got me out of the harbor but it died, it's dead. People are looking at me as they motor by wondering what the heck I'm doing just sitting out here. Weather report says there should be the usual winds, same as yesterday, but they should have been here by now. It is an overcast and pretty gloomy looking day. It has done everything but rain.

"I hope I can have a better report tonight when I get around the island. Feeling pretty good. Put it this way, I bet I could drift to Hawaii.

(Taping outside with the wind's high-pitched whining in the background.) "It is dark and windy; the West End of Catalina Island is still in sight. I have put a reef in my main and have my storm jib up. I headed a little too far south towards the Isthmus and now I am beating towards the West

CHAPTER EIGHT

End. Winds are gusting fifteen to twenty knots but there are no whitecaps yet, which is helping to give me a smooth ride. I am talking from the cockpit as I sail down the coast. I had three meals today. Looking good. *Little Breeze* is doing great. The West End flashing light is visible in the distance on the port beam. I am steering 300 degrees magnetic and after clearing the West End, I plan to turn and steer south-southwest. The boat is self-steering."

Sunday
June 13 – Day 3

LOG
0938 – 1207
33°29'N
118°38'W
No wind. Large west swell.
Hot clear day with large heaps of cumulus clouds to northeast.
Drifting S-SE
1436
33°24'N
118°48'W
Cse – 200° magnetic (M)
Wind out of west 10 – 15 knots with 6-foot swells out of west.
Working jib, full main reaching.
2000
Now drifting to the NE
Wind too strong and took in all sails, let out warp.

DISAPPOINTING FIRST DAYS

Hanging on!
Watch 19 seconds fast.
(As compared with the time tick at WWV Fort Collins, Colorado, for coordinated universal time.)
44 nautical miles daily run
70.3 total nautical miles

TAPE

(An occasional sniffle can be heard as I talk.) "Taping is the only way I can put it in a log entry today. Winds gusting twenty to twenty-five knots. Swell six foot. Approximate position ten miles south-southwest of San Clemente Island. Winds came up really quick and the seas kept building.

"Found a few leaks in the boat that I really didn't count on, but between weather stripping and silicon, she is holding her own. Storm jib up. Still doing three knots. Basically on a south heading. I'm not really feeling all that great. But the sun is out, I am inside and the boat is sailing herself. How long this will last, I don't know. Going to try and get some sleep before night comes when I might have to be diligent and awake for passing ships.

"Tomorrow, hopefully the weather will be a little nicer. Looking for those trades."

Monday
June 14 – Day 4

LOG
2400

CHAPTER EIGHT

SW
wells from north-northwest, 3.6 ft.
One reef in main.
51.2 nautical miles daily run
121.2 total nautical miles

JOURNAL

Had a really rough day yesterday, went through what I would call a gale, but no rain. I was forced to drop all sails and deploy a warp. Basically I used my anchor rode as a warp; it consists of 300 feet of 5/16 inch yacht braid anchor rode with 30 feet of 1/4 inch chain shackled on the end. I let the chain out, over the side off the stern, let all 300 feet of rode out and then tied off the bitter end to a cleat on the transom. I prefer using a warp instead of a sea anchor. Sea anchors are usually deployed from the bow and are meant to keep the boat pointing into the wind and sea while limiting drift. I wanted to drift, especially downwind. I just needed to prevent *Little Breeze* from being hurled broadside to the sea and broached. *Little Breeze* rode the warp really well and I was able to sleep.

I am hungry, but I don't feel like cooking because I don't want to clean and to tell the truth, nothing appeals to me. I feel like I want to throw up, but I am not seasick, just a lump in my stomach. I guess it is my nerves. I was really scared there for a moment when I went up forward to change to a storm jib and the entire bow and half of me went underwater!

For a split-second I thought that this could be it, but the *Little Breeze* just popped right back up through the wave. I finished changing sails and headed back to the cockpit as fast as I could. After a while sailing became useless and so I went back to a warp, which I was glad to have ready. Then I headed into the refuge and comfort of my cabin. Everything from here on out is a first for me. *Little Breeze* has been sailing real well for some time now. I don't ever want to go outside again due to the unpredictable weather.

I had a few leaks last night. I hope I solved them. I can tell already that I brought some foods that I will not use and not enough wool clothing!

Whenever I try to read I get really sleepy.

I am fine and I think I will be as long as I can make progress, stay out of the wind, stay as dry as possible, and most importantly as long as the boat holds up.

TAPE

(More sniffles.) "It is now 6:30 p.m. and so far it has been a real uneventful day of pleasant sailing. Had the sails up all day. The boat has been self-steering quite well on a southwest heading. I was using one of the bungee cord self-steering techniques of running the leeward jib sheet across the cockpit, through a snatch block on the windward gunwale, and then secured the sheet to the cleat on the tiller. Then a second bungee cord is tied from the lee gunwale to another cleat on the tiller for compensating tension. As the winds increase, the pressure on the jib is transferred to the jib sheet, which in turn pulls the tiller to windward and forces

CHAPTER EIGHT

the bow to fall off slightly keeping the speed up. The bungee on the lee rail allows the tiller to have enough resistance to keep the bow from falling off too far. In this way the back and forth forces keep the boat sailing generally on course even with the winds that are not consistent in direction or intensity.

"Things are getting damp inside. It seems like the boat is sweating a bit. Or maybe the hull-to-deck joint is leaking, but I can't tell. I am getting traces of moisture around the inside seam. Not much, but enough to make things a little damp inside here. My nose had been clogged ever since I started this trip. Feeling better today, but still can't get myself to eat much. Today I had a can of beans, a can of fruit cocktail, and pineapple. No sun today, couldn't take a sight. Saw San Clemente Island, I think, very early this morning. Also earlier this morning I saw a freighter loaded with containers that passed across my bow heading east. My navigation has basically been advancing my DR position every four hours. If nothing else, even if I never get reliable sun sights, I can remain relatively confident of my location by frequently advancing my DR position. At noon each day I will transfer the latitude and longitude of the noon DR position to a small scale Pacific Ocean chart (chart #530) for a better perspective of my progress across 2,200 miles of Pacific Ocean.

"On approximately thirty-two degrees north latitude, one hundred nineteen degrees west longitude.

"Days have been good. Nights are the hardest. Have been trying to catch a few zzz's before darkness falls. I have a reef in my main already. Seas are still calm, winds are steady, but you never know when they can shift. Have to be ready for anything out here. I wish I had installed a cabin vent. Things are a little stuffy in here since I keep the drop boards in and the cabin hatch shut at all times. Everything closed up tight is standard safety at sea. All it would take would be for some rogue wave to roll over the stern and into my open cabin; that would ruin all my gear, not to mention could sink us."

CHAPTER NINE

Settling into a Routine

Tuesday
June 15 – Day 5

LOG
0400
32°17'N
119°27'W
Cse – averaging SW
Everything seems the same, cold, cloudy, and visibility about five miles.
0800
Swell 1 – 2 feet northwest.
Wind 5 – 10 knots from the west.
1200
31°55'N
119°46'W
Cse – S magnetic
Sea is calm.
2230
Cse – S magnetic
Self-steering, jib controlling, broad reaching,

CHAPTER NINE

wind and swell from north-northwest.
Wind 8 – 10 knots. Seas 1 – 2 feet.
Watch error 19 seconds fast.
73 nautical miles daily run
194.2 total nautical miles

JOURNAL

I am just now realizing the immensity of the distance I have to cover. My fourth day out of San Pedro and this is just a drop in the bucket. I was getting a bit anxious when I was off San Clemente, the waves were towering over my boat, but *Little Breeze* did real well. She rolled up and over the six- to seven-foot steep swells or shed the water when an occasional wave would break over the bow. I just wish I knew exactly where I was. I haven't been able to take a sight for three days and so all I have are my DR positions. Haven't seen anything but one little bird for days now.

The "self-steering" arrangement leaves me plenty of time to clean up my little space and take care of my needs, but self-steering is only so accurate. Problem is when steering by the apparent wind and then the wind slowly changes, so does my course. I keep a close eye on my compass and later I kind of average the various courses out in my head when it comes time to plot a DR position. Dead Reckoning is all I've been able to do for three days. It sure would be embarrassing if I hit San Diego or Mexico. In other respects things are OK. I would feel even better with a successful sun sight.

TAPE

"It is now noon, approximate latitude thirty-one degrees, fifty-five minutes north, longitude one hundred nineteen degrees, forty-eight minutes west.

"Feeling really good. I had two excellent meals today; I fixed up some eggs for breakfast this morning with melted cheese and chopped onions, salt, pepper, and bread with jam. I munched that entire tasty dish down. And for dinner I made my special green beans ala Michael Mann recipe by adding a small can of cream of chicken soup with Rice-a-Roni. Really good stuff boy.

"Self-steering all day. Heading basically south. Trying to find those trades any day. Putting in a good day; I should make better than a sixty-mile run today. Better, better, better. In fact, I had fifty miles in by my four o'clock plot.

"Doing really well. Skies overcast; how I wish I knew when the skies will clear because I can't take any sights. DR, DR, DR—dear, dear, dear!"

Wednesday June 16 – Day 6

LOG

0400
30°59'N
119°58'W
Cse – S
Main reefed once, jib still controlling.
Have used 1 ¾ gallons of water.
0800

CHAPTER NINE

30°44'N
120°02'W
Cse – W to SW
Turned to a west-southwest heading.
Swell pounding boat from northwest.
Wind is 10 – 15 knots from the west.
1200
30°34'N
120°W
Cse – still S
Having trouble with some slight leaks coming in under the forward lip of the hatch.
2000
30°14'N
120°34'W
Everything going well,
but clouds still prevent taking a sight.
Watch error 19 – 20 seconds fast against the chronometer.
76 nautical miles daily run
270.2 total nautical miles traveled

JOURNAL

It is noon and the darn lead on the forward edge of the companionway slide still lets in the water that crashes over the top of cabin. Everything else going as planned.

Feeling the effects of the wind and dampness, my little tickle and cough is going deeper into my throat and becoming sour tasting. I can tell that if I don't do something now it could really become a problem. I've made myself a pot of herbal tea with bits of cinnamon sticks and a teaspoon of honey. Plus, I took an antibiotic capsule Dad gave me. I hate using them so soon but I have to lick this right away. I have been getting plenty of rest, it is just the dampness. No sun for three days. In a way that is good because I don't get sun burned, but then I cannot dry anything out.

Today I need to check and replace, if necessary, the batteries in my flashlight and in the tape player.

It is during the night I feel so small and insignificant when looking into the deep dark blackness all around me. My mast head light is a beacon in the heavens. The invisible breeze pushes my boat forever and unceasingly onward to an unforeseen shore. I wish I had been able to get a hold of a Coast Pilot publication for Hawaii. Aaah!—Hawaii, in the beginning a dream but now a goal and adventure.

Made really good time today, over sixty miles. Better than my average. By tomorrow morning I should have gone 300 miles since leaving Huntington Beach.

I am starting to fall into a regular pattern and a daily routine, as long as the weather is at least fair. I have broken the day into what I feel are comfortable four-hour watches.

2400 – 0400 – "Late Night Watch": plot midnight DR position, maybe read, listen to music, write, but mainly sleep. While lying back in my cozy cabin, wedged between duffle bags, I can read by flashlight. I have to be careful not to fall asleep with the light on and waste my batteries.

0400 – 0800 – "Sunrise Watch": plot 4:00 a.m. DR position, sleep until dawn and begin the day. Watch the beautiful sunrise and make a thermos of hot water for my instant coffee. Assess *Little Breeze* and make sure she is in good order and that nothing came apart during the night. Also, conjure up a little breakfast.

0800 – 1200 – "Morning Watch": general maintenance, plot 8:00 a.m. position, make any course changes if necessary, start cleaning my cabin, and taking care of standing rigging, which includes adjusting turnbuckles, checking for loose hardware and other exterior fittings. Maybe make a lunch if I am hungry.

1200 – 1600 – "Afternoon Watch": plot noon DR position and if all is well then the rest of the afternoon is mine to sleep, read, do general grooming, write, and listen to music. What else is there?

1600 – 2000 – "Sundown Watch": plot 4:00 p.m. DR position and make dinner, the usual. This is a special time of night when I sit in the cabin (with the drop boards in, but with the cabin slide open a bit) and gaze into the night as the skies darken and change color—a time where again I make a thermos of hot water for coffee. This is a good time when I reflect on the day and take a mental inventory of my situation. How are my food and water stores doing? How is the boat holding up? How am I holding up?

2000 – 2400 – "Evening Watch": plot 8:00 p.m. DR position. Before I lose all the light I plot my position on the General Ocean chart and make entries in ship's log.

Well there you have it, the day in a life of a person solo at sea. Notice not a lot of time allotted for sailing. Well, I put an hour in there somewhere to trim the sails and reset the self-steering. With the jib control setup I don't even have to leave the cabin to make course corrections. I just reach out and give a yank on the jib sheet.

It is currently three o'clock in the afternoon and I can't believe that it is the same day. I have been reading since seven o'clock this morning. I had a breakfast of some oatmeal and for lunch sausage and cheese sandwiches. At least I have my appetite and the cold and sore throat have gone away for now. I think I have gotten over the fright of the first few days, being alone at sea, in high seas, and now the waiting and watching begins. Waiting to see what happens next, like another storm or a ship or something, and watching myself slowly deteriorate. My scalp is already flaky and itching. I would wash, but there has been no sun since San Clemente Island and it is a little cold outside. I haven't been able to go to the bathroom for a couple of days so I've started to eat a lot of raisins in hopes of making it natural. If not, some Ex-lax® will do the trick.

I am comfortable in my quarters lying back on the dark blue V-berth cushions, which are three-inch thick foam covered with vinyl, and stare up at the stark white fiberglass interior. I use duffle bags stuffed with clothing as padding against the cold damp sides of the cabin. I wish I could take everything out, clean, and repack it again. The surroundings will eventually start to close in if I let them.

If only I could take a good sight and confirm my position, I would sleep a little more easily. It is not as easy as I thought it would be to use a sextant out here on a bobbing little boat in ten-foot seas. If the skies are continuously overcast then I am out of luck using the sun to obtain a noon fix. I wish I'd taken the time to learn the additional steps needed to obtain a fix by using the stars!

The nights are the hardest. You look up and out and it is black—I mean BLACK! But the wind still blows and you still sail on. I can see how in the old days it would be easy to imagine sailing to the edge of the world. But, ah, what could you find there?

One last thing that might be of interest, at night when I do sleep, I dream of people on board, but they're not really on board. They are just people giving me advice. I picture an island, maybe Hawaii, and visualize how it may look as I approach it. I don't think I'm hallucinating, just actively dreaming to make up for the lack of activity during the day. I also have the usual dreams of people I know on the mainland, familiar faces and places. I seem to always be awake in the dream yet always neutral at the same time.

Dad cautioned me about "sensory deprivation" that can cause anxiety, depression or hallucinations. In the absence of human company, solo sailors (like Josh Slocum, Gerry Spiess and Robert Manry) would often subconsciously or consciously ease the anxiety by concocting an imaginary friend. I remember reading a book by Josh Slocum, the first man to solo circumnavigate the world, and he had dreams of a mysterious "pilot" who would take the helm at night. My daily conversations on these tape recordings should provide me enough stimuli so my dreams won't become overwhelming.

Thursday
June 17 – Day 7

LOG

0045
30°05'N
120°46'W
Variable course 240° – 210° magnetic.
Winds light then gusty from the north then northwest.
0519
29°52'N
120°52'W
A definite green glow floating by.
0800
29°43'N
120°56'W
1200
29°32'N
121°W
Heading west as best I can.
Winds light and variable from the west.
Have to start heading west.
Where are those trades? Close reach to beating.
Main sheet controlling.
Need those northeast winds.
1313
29°37'N
121°17'W
Cse – 230° True
This is the first sun sight position. Really close.
If it's accurate then I am doing well.
1600

CHAPTER NINE

Heading 220° magnetic. Broad reaching.
Wind off the starboard quarter.
1800
No change in course.
Wind is backing to the northwest.
I must begin heading west soon.
Where are those northeast winds?
2000
Approximate Position
29°20'N
121°24'W
Cse – S
Nearest I can head is SW 210° magnetic or NW 310° magnetic.
Where is the happy medium?
71.7 nautical miles daily run
341.9 total nautical miles traveled

TAPE

"I am getting down to the 30th parallel. It has been blowing hard ever since eight o'clock last night. Still left the working jib up and one reef in my main. My *Little Breeze* has been zinging along. Still cloudy. Still haven't been able to take a sight. Getting a little discouraged on that point. Would sure like to see if I am even close to my DR and not just doing circles out here.

"It was a pretty interesting evening last night when I saw some thick, neon green fluorescence in the water, plankton probably and other little goodies swimming by. An abundance of tiny microscopic organisms cause this eerie event. When disturbed by my bow, each gives off a brief flash of light with this brilliant result; a very impressive display for someone out here alone on an endless ocean.

"Having problems with my electrical system. The main fuse is not making a very good connection so I am getting intermittent flashing on all my instruments. It was something that I thought I had taken care of before, but I didn't and will probably have to pay for it sooner or later. I'll make some repairs on it today as soon as I get in a little calmer seas.

"I have been letting *Little Breeze* run as hard as she can and she seems to be taking it all in stride. The inside is doing really great. Holding together just fine. I am doing just fine. It was getting a little monotonous yesterday. The same old intense repetitive motion. But today the boat seems to be moving in all kinds of different directions.

"I haven't sighted anyone or anything since I left the Channel Islands, just small birds that fly in and out of the troughs of the swells. That is about the only living thing I've seen.

"Heading on a southwest course. Approximately three knots. Averaging three to four knots this trip so far. Yesterday, I put in over seventy miles in less than twenty-four hours which was fantastic!

"Have slowed down a bit because I have been sleeping more and I am not keeping track of the boat. I feel the boat, I am part of the boat, I am in tune with the boat and its motion, and I know how it's riding in relation to the way the swells hit it. I feel good when I know how the sails are adjusted without looking at them. I feel really good about the boat. I just wish I knew for sure where I am."

CHAPTER TEN

Baffling Winds

Friday
June 18 – Day 8

LOG
0024
Cse – S
Light winds all over.
Have sighted what could be a fishing boat
about three miles north of me.
Two white lights separated and high off the water.
Under one light, several green square lights in rows
(could be starboard running lights)
with one red light towards one end
(could be a port light)
but one other white light is detached,
cannot see anything under it.
0455
28°56'N
121°32'W
Cse – Variable 225° – 185° magnetic
0800

CHAPTER TEN

28°47'N
121°34'W
Cse – 200° – 219° magnetic
I am beginning to feel a little disheartened
by the fact that I can't head any farther west
without continuing to head north.
1200
28°40'N
121°37'W
Cse – Variable 170° – 210° magnetic
If I can't get west 250° – 260° magnetic by
tomorrow I will have to head 320°
Watch error 20 seconds fast.
1313
320° magnetic
It's really slow going.
1600
28°42'N
121°53'W, MPP (Most probable position)
The horizon was a little cloudy
but the sight could not have been closer.
2200
After screwing around all day,
tacking northwest and southwest,
the wind seemed like it was coming around
to the northeast then died—DIED!
Although, 57.2 miles were traveled,
it might as well have been a circle.
57.2 nautical miles daily run
399.1 total nautical miles traveled

JOURNAL

Today is my eighth day at sea, if you count the day over in San Pedro. All is well on board except I fear that I am losing some water from the bottles I packed in the forward locker. I will make an attempt to go over my water today. Actually I am not using as much water as I thought I would. I haven't even used two-and-a-half gallons so far. I figured three-and-a-half gallons per week.

Yesterday was both a good and a bad day. The good parts were that I was able to take a well-deserved and much needed constitutional. Also, the sun came out in patches and I was able to take a sight that put me about twenty miles west-southwest of my DR position. Now if it was a good sight and my DR position was half as close, then most likely I'm in a thirty- to fifty-mile radius of my most probable position (MPP). I tried another sight four-and-a-half hours later. It calculated out all right, but if I were to use it as a running fix (Rfx) then it would have put me about seventy miles southwest of my DR at that time. I feel that the sight was too soon so I chose to stick with my DR. The bad part was that I wanted to start heading farther west but the wind seems to still be from that direction. I may have to head a little northwest to get in some westing. I'm already below 29° latitude but only around 120° longitude.

I hope all is well at home. I hope my sister Laurel had a good graduation on Wednesday.

I wonder what people are thinking and saying about me. Probably that I'm crazy, foolish, unwise and a bit impulsive. Maybe they're right. But then they are not witness to the awesome beauty and mystery that I have come to know and respect out here. The cloud formations are an endless design. The sea itself changes in shape and form as if an invisible hand were sculpting them for my amusement. It's as if I am the only one in this world being taught a lesson that I have yet to be aware of.

TAPE

(Speech is slowing.) "Another day. I had a chance to take a sight yesterday which was close. And in view of everything, as far as navigation, I am heading steadily south and not getting the westerly movement I would like.

"Things are pretty slow going right now. I took the opportunity this morning to go over my lockers and check everything out. Looks real good. Still have roughly over thirty-two gallons of water left. Plenty of food (canned goods). I finally used up my first can of cooking fuel yesterday. One can lasted seven days, maybe more.

"*Little Breeze* is shipshape except for some curious drainage I keep getting in my cabin footwell. There isn't enough in my sump for the bilge pump to bail out. The lockers had moisture in the bottoms of them but nothing major. Seems like just a lot of condensation from the warm moist air in my cabin and the cold sea against my hull.

"The skies have been cloudy the whole time, except for yesterday it broke for half the day. Put on my first change of clothes yesterday which felt incredibly good. (Probably a good thing this is a solo voyage.)

"Looks to me like I have another 2,000 miles left to go. Where are those trades? I hope the winds start to shift at least from the north, but no, they are still out of the west.

"I wonder what everyone's doing on the mainland right now. I know I wish I were on the mainland now. Everything is going well and I do feel good. It's just that I am getting a little discouraged about my navigation.

"Started up the old seagull today to exercise it (British Seagull, outboard motor—only one quart of fuel in the tank). She ran like a champ. For safe keeping I rewrapped her in the three plastic trash bags, strapped her with duct tape, and lashed her back in the upright and locked position on her motor mount.

"I am going to get some sleep now. Maybe the sun will come out and I will be able to take a sight.

(Later that day.) "I am in my cabin right now. I seem to be making some forward motion.

"My cabin, my little cubical I call my home! Everything I own, everything I need, and everything keeping me together is in here. I have my little happy face button pinned up above me with my navigational aids, lighter, and pencils. There are my two gear hammocks swinging from the overhead on both sides of the cabin with the basics, cigarettes, flashlight, gloves, and cassette tapes. My sleeping bag and everything I want to stay dry is up forward. My first aid kit, lifejacket, towel, and foul weather gear at hand. Food and water are stored under both the cockpit and the lockers below me.

"My little time capsule going from the life I knew, loved, played around in, and took for granted, to the life of the future, the life I am living now, today, and the life that I have a lot more appreciation for. Putting myself in this sort of position has made me a bit more wary. I will definitely think harder next time I try a stunt like this, but there is no turning back now. Everything is going great but another thirty to forty days! Oh God—No!"

Saturday June 19 – Day 9

LOG

0230
Cse – West, wind slight from the northeast, steering by hand.
0530
Cse – 284° magnetic
Tied off tiller so that I could sleep, awoke heading southeast.
0600
Wind really cold out of the northwest.
0954
MPP
28°47'N
122°08'W
Sunshine today and wind north by northwest. Maybe I can get a running fix (Rfx) today.
0954 – 1553
28°38'N Rfx
122°44'W
Cse – Variable 240° – 270° magnetic
Three sights. Couldn't be better. West swell. Winds steady out of the northwest all day.
2114
Cse – 230° magnetic
Have started to fall off a bit.

Watch error 20 – 21 seconds fast.
41.8 nautical miles daily run (Bad!)
449 total nautical miles traveled

JOURNAL

You can never predict what lies ahead on the ocean, even hour to hour. Last night around ten o'clock, the wind started to come around from the east. My sails billowed as if they wanted to start a downwind run. I started to get excited that maybe I had found the trades! I sat in the cockpit for about two hours hoping that the winds would continue from the east so I could then pull out my twin headsails. Well, the wind slowly died to nothing and soon I was becalmed on a lifeless dead sea. Nothing left to do but pull in the sails and make a comforting cup of hot chocolate.

When I tried to sleep I was plagued with dreams that made me uneasy and I would break out in a cold sweat. I figured I was in a high pressure area with a lot of humidity. I should try to trace the weather records to see if what was reported or predicted was what was actually occurring.

Back to change of events. I awoke this morning with a light breeze coming off to starboard. I hoisted sail and ghosted along with the tiller tied. I jumped down to get a few more winks when I was awakened around 6:00 a.m. with the boat jibing about. Soon I had a steady breeze from the west-northwest and I was able to set a good west-southwest course and started my day.

The first order of business was to fix my cabin light which had failed the night before. After two hours of aggravation

CHAPTER TEN

testing this and that, moving gear here and there, to get at wires, I was able to get all lights working—what a relief. Just as I finished, the sun broke through and I grabbed the sextant for a sight which later calculated out very well. The sight put me within ten miles of my best guess position after all this drifting and sailing on a deserted Pacific Ocean!

Before I worked out the sight I took advantage of the sun and light air to give myself a well-deserved shampoo and washcloth bath. I just ended up getting naked in the cockpit and pouring pails of sea water over me; I used a special soap that lathered in seawater. Then I took a very sparse amount of fresh water on a rag to rinse the sea salt off.

Boy did that feel good! I just don't think I can bring myself to actually jump in, over the side, and swim near the boat for a bath. Another nightmare would be for me to be in the water and have the boat sail off and leave me to a terrible fate. I know I could tie off to a line, but then there are the "sea creatures" that might get me.

After covering myself in baby powder and trimming my beard I put out some clothes to dry on a line and made a grand lunch. Two healthy sized ham sandwiches with mustard, ketchup, and Velveeta cheese. It looks like it will be ham in the Top Raman for dinner and ham in the eggs for breakfast. Life is tough. But seriously, I am starting to get a bit lonely and upset that I didn't bring more cassette tapes.

Anyway, for dinner I fixed a great meal of mashed potatoes with melted Velveeta cheese and chopped ham, topped off with a can of sliced pears on the side—mmm, good! Food has such a flavor, such meaning out here. You savor the thought, the preparation, and the consumption.

But alas, night falls upon this soul with no one to share this experience with. I am content. I wonder how Gerry Spiess made out on his trip to Hawaii in his 10-foot *Yankee Girl* last year. In comparison my 15-foot *Little Breeze* would seem like a yacht. A big black cloud layer hovers to the north. I hope it doesn't move down and spoil my view of those stars you never see in the cities. What better entertainment than to lie back comfortably in my cabin and gaze up into infinity.

TAPE

"Nine days now. Yesterday was a pretty disappointing day. I couldn't get anywhere with the boat. I wasted the whole day trying to do some westing when I should have kept on an easier course.

"Right now I am heading approximately 254 degrees magnetic. Going on a pretty good clip, close reached. Self-steering since this morning. Took a good sun sight, hopefully I can get another sun sight later this afternoon for a Rfx.

"Been dozing and reading. Been writing quite a bit. Everything is going real well. I had some trouble with my electrical this morning but after some agonizing hours working on it I got it fixed. Last night, I was becalmed from about ten o'clock until six o'clock this morning. Sadly I lost eight hours of travel time. Another thirty days maybe.

"Today has been the best day so far. Beautiful in all respects. And it is at dusk, when the day slips away into the night, when I feel like I am in on the threshold of something infinitely great in the universe. Sea and sky blend together to tingle and excite the senses. I feel like I want to scream out "I am ME! I am here! With all of you! We are one!" but then the quiet splashing of the swell against my fiberglass *Little Breeze* is calming."

Sunday
June 20 – Day 10

LOG
0228
Cse – 180° – 200° magnetic
Wind died then shifted. Thick marine layer,
light and variable winds all around the dial.
Note: I can tell that the first of my two 12-Volt
batteries is starting to go dead already,
but these are still shipping lanes and I wanted to
keep my running lights on from sunset to sunrise.
0750
28°36'N
123°W
Cse – Variable 210° – 240°
For the past few hours I have been jibing in circles.
The winds are so screwy at night
and I am too lazy to pull down the sails.
I just tie off the tiller.
Broad reaching, jib controlling.
1442
28°21'N, MPP
123°43'W
Cse – 250°

Course will be True Cse unless otherwise noted.
1745
Cse – 260°
Wind has picked up and has been blowing for about 2 ½ hours. The boat is powering through the swell comfortably. Would like to do this for a few days and nights.
1900
28°17'N
123°58'W
Cse – 250°
Put in a reef.
2230
Cse – 250° – 235°
Shook out reef. Best night run in three days. Keep going baby!
55.3 nautical miles daily run
496.2 total nautical miles traveled

JOURNAL

Well here it is only ten days out and I am already running low on three very important commodities; 12-volt power, battery power and smokes. Because Stan loaned me his tape player I figured I wouldn't need a third car battery. Well, I can tell by the lights dimming when using two or more instruments that my first car battery is getting low. I will try not to use this power for a whole week, except for an emergency. So my tape recorded messages will be cut down a bit.

Now back to Stan's tape player. I like music so I guess

CHAPTER TEN

I've been playing it a lot and last night I fell asleep with it on. That was the end of those C cell batteries, but I still have two more replacement sets. Good thinking, brains! No more music except for emergencies. The rotten part is I brought a lot of 9-volt and AA batteries for the Radio Shack TimeKube (for radio time tick) and calculator, which I hardly use. The last battery powered items are the flashlight, and the strobe flashlight. Well, I'm pretty good on D batteries, but next time I'll get fifty of each like I had wanted. Those things cost a fortune.

As for cigarettes, I thought I wouldn't really want any, but it is so nice to have one after a cup of coffee or to kill time during night watches. I only brought one carton and I am down to seven packs. There are one hundred forty smokes to last maybe thirty to forty days. Either way the figures are discouraging to say the least. When I started the trip, I didn't feel good so I didn't smoke much. Now that I'm feeling better, I am back to smoking almost a pack a day; I'll have to cut down.

Today is Father's Day and Dad will be getting the letter I wrote before I departed. I don't remember what I wrote, but I know, as with all my letters to Dad, I tried to be wise, prolific, and profound because maybe he'd think Michael knows what he's doing.

This trip is supposed to help me think of my past and future, but all I can think about is the present and getting to Hawaii as quickly and safely as possible. I really don't know what I want to do as a profession, as a way to meet life's little demands, like room and board. I like my hobbies which mostly deal with the sea—sailing, scuba diving and fishing when I can. I would like working on the ocean. My job as a Marine Technician has been the closest I've come, but they laid me off. No work and last I heard things are crumbling down at MBC. And we can't count that one month I worked on the broadbill fishing boat the summer after graduating from Catalina. I just didn't want to leave the island yet.

Sailing on commercial ships has never appealed to me. To sit on greasy, stinky freighters is not what I had in mind, especially as a deck hand. I would like to work on the sea but maybe as a navigator. This is one possibility I will look into if I am successful in navigating my way to Hawaii. If I can't do that then I need not worry about any of the above.

> **Dad** — Happy Father's Day!
>
> *Frances* — Thank you for the food, clothes and caring.
>
> **Mom** — I hope you are happy and well.
>
> **Mike, Stacy and Jeremiah** — I love you all.
>
> **Laurel** — I love you too and be all you can be.
>
> **Marshall, Warren, Anne and Nichol** — Good luck and live happy.
>
> **Marc** — Thanks, I could never have gotten this far without your help.
>
> **Jack** — You old son of a gun, thanks for the use of the camera and I hope you keep out of trouble.
>
> **Hey Whit** — Thanks for everything.
>
> **Stan** — I'm doing all right.
>
> **Jerry** — If I don't make it the *Little Breeze* has already proved herself.

CHAPTER TEN

> ***Jimmy*** — It was nice working with you.
>
> ***Liz*** — I hope you are thinking about me.
>
> ***Pete*** — Long time no hear. Believe me I thought we would be friends and in close contact for years. But now you're married with kids. All this I was hoping to share with you.

Monday
June 21 – Day 11

LOG

0123

Cse – Variable

Wind went dead. Light and variable all around.

Will make something to eat and deal with it.

0400

Turned out to be a hard night again;

I couldn't get to sleep and the wind died on me.

What a waste of time and lost miles.

0847 – 0919

27°58'N

124°06'W

Cse – SE and have come around to 200° magnetic

Wind is now from the west-southwest.

Wind real light, seas calm, swell almost due north.

1200 – 1500

Cse – about the same

Wind light but still making 3 – 3 ½ knots.

Considering putting up the genoa.

1800

27°45'N
125°18'W
Cse – 225°
Wind picking up in the afternoon as usual to 12 – 15 knots. Choppy seas, occasional whitecaps, full sail.
2030 – 2329
Becoming lighter air, as usual at night, but still keeping us moving.
50.5 nautical miles daily run
546.7 total nautical miles traveled

TAPE

"It's been eleven days and that could mean I'm one-third the way there, one-fourth the way there, or one-fifth the way there. The way things have been going lately I think it is towards the latter.

"The last four nights I have been becalmed from six to eight hours cutting my miles down to forty per day. Variable winds frustrate me in the morning and then the winds pick up in the afternoon and stay fresh into the evening. By 10:30 to 11:00 p.m. I am awakened by the clash of my rig jibing and bashing all over.

"The only personal fatigue I can notice is in my inability to contend with this light and variable wind and in keeping the boat moving under any amount of wind. I get frustrated and start yelling at *Little Breeze*, the rig, the ocean and everything else.

"A few more days before I make another entry. So hang in there, I sure will."

CHAPTER ELEVEN

BECALMED-WHAT DO I DO NOW?

Tuesday
June 22 – Day 12

LOG
0437
Cse – 195°
I awoke around 0115 to find the boat
on a northerly heading.
Have to correct to a more southerly course.
I hate this. Now I have to figure out drift for
sailing north for who knows how long to
correct my DR position.
At least I got to sleep five hours straight.
0700
Ghosting.
1030
I guess I am within five to ten miles
of my last position. Totally becalmed!
I lashed my oars to the cockpit coamings,
but I couldn't row for any longer than a half hour.
If this should go on all day
I think I will be in a sad frame of mind.

CHAPTER ELEVEN

*Well at least I can do my laundry and take a bath;
it's becoming a much needed ritual.
The sea is calm.
I think there is a current running
from the northwest. Overcast skies.
The water is still very cold—help!*
1300
*Drifting south.
Still light air from the southwest.*
1600
Approximate
27°28'N
124°32'W
*Cse – Variable 125° – 210°
Still light air but we are moving. Thank heavens.*
1622
27°28'N
124°52'W MPP
*This sight was taken under cloudy skies,
but it was within twenty miles of DR,
which I consider a good sight.
Although all my sights have been almost
right on the latitude, my sights keep pushing me
west fifteen to twenty miles.
I just hope I am close.
I wish more than anything
I could get an accurate fix.*
30.5 nautical miles daily run (Very discouraging.)
577.2 total nautical miles traveled

JOURNAL

It is a cool, quiet morning. The overcast skies turn a calming pink as the dawn approaches. The sea surface is smooth and mirror like. Time stands still for a moment. The twelfth day begins.

And as quietly as it began, another day comes to a close, following the sun as it sinks into the west. The gentle splashing of a sailboat's bow as it makes its way through the water is musical. All is at peace in my world on the sea, on my *Little Breeze*.

P.S. Earlier today had a fright as I was becalmed until one o'clock this afternoon. I thought to myself this would be the end of my patience as I floundered on a sea that resembled a massive pond. But praise be to the God of the wind that took heed of my pleas and granted a quiet blow.

Wednesday
June 23 – Day 13

LOG

0023
Becalmed.
WE 21 seconds fast.
0830
27°10'N
125°6'W
Cse – S
0930
Cse – 213°
Hoisted my genoa this morning.

CHAPTER ELEVEN

1130
Becalmed!
Drifting south. Dropped sails.
1217
27°9'N
125°18'W MPP
1300
Cse – Averaging 125°
Sails up.
1500
Cse – Averaging 215° – 225°
Took genoa down, put up working jib.
1636
27°N
125°24'W Rfx—real close
Cse – 220°
2030
Cse – 195°
Winds becoming light from north-northwest.
29 nautical miles daily run
606.2 total nautical miles traveled

JOURNAL

Please wind, come early! Pilot charts indicate a twelve mile per day current running south-southwest. I have been drifting for eight hours so I figure four miles to the south. After breakfast I observed a small pod of pilot whales breaching approximately 200 yards off the starboard, heading south-southwest. So I am not alone!

Have been barely moving on this course for two to three hours. If the swell from the north wouldn't make the boom jibe so hard everything would be gravy. I will need to have between 700 – 840 miles logged by Saturday to be somewhat on schedule.

I am becoming very disappointed that I haven't been able to do a sixty-mile day in five days. I have to average at least fifty miles per day to be there in forty-eight days. I would gladly stay up day and night. In fact, I do. The winds come and go. The wind blows for a few hours in the morning then stops until one o'clock in the afternoon. Then the wind slowly builds to climax in the evening and then dies again between nine o'clock and midnight. What am I doing wrong? What can I do?

Not a plane can be seen because of the incessant clouds. Not a ship or boat have I seen since the Channel Islands. Have I made a mistake? What can I do but sit and drift and sail when I can? Things, I feel, are not going as they should. Where are those trades? I would be comforted by either continuous winds or the passing of a ship. Even to catch a fish would help.

Night comes and again I'll sit and stare out on the placid horizon.

Thursday
June 24 – Day 14

LOG

0011

CHAPTER ELEVEN

Cse – 240°
0430
Cse – 200°
Until I get some 50 – 60 mile days I am going on half rations. I can't wait to put up my twins.
Light breeze all night. Sails are still up anyway.
0830
26°41'N
125°39'W
Becalmed.
Slight drift southwest.
1130
Cse – 240°
Slight wind out of the NE. Could this be it (trades)?
Hoping, so I can put up my twins.
Not enough wind to keep them full right now,
but I am still hoping.
Swell out of the north, sea is calm.
1633
Cse – SW
Hauled down the twins—nothing.
Back to main and jib.
Wind out of the northwest again.
WE 22 seconds fast
1749 – 2135
26°25'N
126°04'W approximate
Cse – 255°
Already down to a crawl.
Soon I will have to take down sail.

I will leave them up as long as the VDO sum log clicks off the tenths of a mile and my sails and boom don't bang themselves to death.
I need a steady breeze.
The moon is new and at a crescent.
Stars are like buckshot in the sky.
Second stove fuel canister gone.
0035
Cse – 300°
Wind came up from the northeast while I was sleeping.
Don't know how long I have been on this course. Cannot hold on any course west unless I put up twins and I just went through that today.
Will see how she blows come morning.
26.4 nautical miles daily run
632.6 total nautical miles traveled

JOURNAL

Had an interesting day today—no, I didn't sail sixty miles. First thing, I ate; then took a bath. As I was finishing cleaning up I noticed something odd. The boat was pointing southwest but I felt a breeze coming from over the stern. Could this be it, I thought to myself. Well, nothing else was going on, so I put up the twin jibs. The breeze was so light and inconsistent that I didn't get anywhere. Around three o'clock the usual afternoon breeze out of the west-northwest started to blow so, I pulled down the twins and folded them and then hoisted the working jib.

CHAPTER ELEVEN

I am on a broad reach now. Wind out of the north. I'm heading west. The sea is calm. The sun that baked today is finally cooling down. A little cream of mushroom soup and some corn for dinner—and so it goes.

TAPE

"About ready to finish up the old dinner here. Sunset will be in a few minutes and boy it's going to be beautiful tonight. Sun came out today hotter than a two-dollar pistol. Not a cloud in the sky.

"Sea calm except for the little ripples being caused by the light breeze. No wind today or yesterday. I have been getting freaky winds at night, which is better than nothing. I have made a little over two hundred miles since Saturday. I almost had a nor'easter today. But they didn't come through and after all the trouble of putting up my twins and hoping and praying, I ended up pulling them down. There sure are a lot of sails on this little boat for one lone sailor to fold. Next time I pull them out, because it took me a while to fold them, the wind has to be howling!

"To put up the twin headsails is a balancing act. I must first make sure the sheet-to-tiller self-steering, with the mainsail only, is balanced so that I can move forward onto the bow. While crouching on the bow and keeping my balance as the boat pitches and rolls in the slight swell, I must (1) fasten the twin headsails to the forestay (leaving the working jib hanked on, lowered and strapped on deck), (2) attach the whisker poles (mounted forward on the mast) to the two clews, (3) attach the bungee downhauls to the poles, and (4) move back to the cockpit all in one smooth maneuver. Having accomplished the fastening of the twins, I hope and pray that as I raise these sails from the cockpit (all my halyards and sheets lead to the cockpit), that the sails fill with wind so that the whisker poles lift unobstructed into position and finally pull tight against the bungee downhauls. But this would not be for us tonight; not enough wind and not from the right direction.

"I am heading right for the sun. It is a lovely sight. The horizon is sharp, crystal clear and distinct in every direction. Barely a swell. The breeze is starting to pick up—thank you very much.

"If I could just do more miles a day I would be in a lot better frame of mind.

"To Stan—haven't caught any fish yet. I really didn't spend a lot of time preparing for fishing. Most of my energy was spent on sailing modifications to *Little Breeze*, food, and navigation. I just grabbed a bunch of lures at the Longs Drug store and some steel leaders. Fishing was basically attaching a lure to a leader and the leader to a fifty-foot one-eighth-inch line attached to a three-foot piece of bungee cord tied to the transom. I put out five lures on different mornings and when I pulled the lines in each afternoon eventually I had no lures left. So much for fishing!

"Arrr, Matey! Nothing like a cup of hot tea and honey and a smoke after a good hearty meal to make a man feel like a real man. God, what am I doing out here?

"I'll look back on this and be proud and wiser for the wear and tear. I *hope* I'm able to think back on this.

"I think I headed too far south at first because I haven't seen one ship; nothing, period. Today I was watching the skies but didn't see any planes either. I figure the great circle route is, maybe 200 miles to the north. Maybe a little advice to the next man trying to do this, the novice sailor, is to talk to a few more people who have sailed it. I don't think I talked to enough people and those I did were racers and they make the crossing from Los Angeles to Hawaii in eight days.

"There is a race I read about, San Francisco to Honolulu, which left on the nineteenth, that is a single-handed race. They should be about halfway by now.

"I am heading south, putting myself farther from Hawaii; still looking for the trades. I have to head west—more west.

"A few months before my departure, I thought and dreamed everyday about what it would be like out here alone on the high seas. Well, I knew what water looked like, I knew what sky and sun looked like, and I knew the thrill and exhilaration of a boat plowing through the water. But now as I sleep here at night, I can think of nothing else but to pull up at that dock (wherever that may be on the islands) tying off the boat, racing up the gangway, and jumping on mother earth, kissing the ground, and falling fast asleep on the first patch of grass I find.

"Everything is going really well and sixty days doesn't bother me except for I am running out of important supplies. A bigger boat could get more speed out of this breeze. Right now I am clicking off two point four knots. Will probably get some wind around midnight.

"I wonder if these are the doldrums. The way I pictured the ocean it would be blowing twenty knots nonstop, indefinitely.

"I wonder what is going on back on the mainland. I

wonder if Los Angeles is still there, or if the "Big One" has happened yet.

"Oh, look at the size of those fifteen- to twenty-foot swells! I guess the seas are a little bit larger than I thought.

"I may be sorry for saying this, but a good thirty-knot gale would sure be a welcomed change of pace right now. It would add a little more excitement to the atmosphere on board here. The first days out I had good strong winds twenty-four hours a day and I had a couple of seventy-mile days there. If the winds had kept up I could be halfway there by now. I guess the tape recorder batteries will be depleted soon so I had better go."

Coffee time in my Little Breeze

(Opposite) Approaching storm, Working with the sails, Self-steering technique

CHAPTER TWELVE

WE'VE HIT THE TRADES!

Friday
June 25 – Day 15

LOG

0141
Cse – 225°
Finally, wind out of the northeast at approximately 7 knots. Twins are up, self-steering and making 2 ½ knots.
0805
Cse – 240°
I can't believe she sailed the rest of the night without any problems. Will adjust rig and practice reefing twin jibes today.
1040
26°15'N
126°56'W MPP
Cse – 240°
Looking good! Wind and swell out of the east.
1520
Tried to plot a running fix, but the advanced line of

CHAPTER TWELVE

position (LOP) and this morning's LOP are parallel and do not cross. Will take another sight in a couple of hours—if the sun is still out.

1727
26°04'N
127°07'W Rfx
Becalmed. Drifting southwest.
Twins down, winds died, swells still following; current appears out of the east.
1752
Cse – 225° – 235°
Light wind from the northeast, twins up.
1945
Cse – 210°
Winds still light and variable north by northeast. Having trouble trimming sails.
Not enough air to keep sails full.
2011
Cse – 260°
Wind picking up out of the northeast.
Following the sunset.
2250
Breeze light.
41.2 nautical miles daily run
(Not so good but better than the last few days.)
673.8 total nautical miles traveled

JOURNAL

It happened. And wouldn't you know it was after

midnight. At around 1:30 in the morning, I had noticed *Little Breeze* picking up speed while I was sleeping. I looked up at the interior compass to find she was driving northwest. When I had gone to sleep around 9:30 p.m. I had her on a reach, jib sheet controlling, with a north-northwest breeze. The wind had come up without warning and veering to the east. I got up, and to my satisfaction, had the boat rigged with twin headsails and self-steering in about thirty minutes. When I have the twins up I always have the mainsail down. It's 8:45 a.m. and we are still trucking along. Alright! "We've hit the trades!"

Time—time, I think, has no definition traveling the high seas. There is only night and day, wind and calm, clouds or clear skies. What should I be thinking at this moment? What should I be writing? I feel that I know what I am to contemplate and there are words and ideas to be scribed. But my mind becomes boggled and my hand falters with the pen. Does everything have meaning—only when you make it so.

Saturday June 26 – Day 16

LOG
0400
Cse – 210°
Breeze steady northeast 5 – 7 knots.
0730
Wind very light.
Sea calm, skies overcast.

CHAPTER TWELVE

1230
Cse – W
Very light breeze, swells coming from the south.
1700
Down to a crawl.
Weather clear and hot again today.
At least I am moving.
Hope for a good breeze again tonight.
1746
Cse – 215°
Picking up a little bit, winds more from the north, hard time keeping her west.
2000
25°49'N
127°44'W
Cse – Variable 225° – 240°
Took down the port jib whisker pole and brought it in tight. I let the starboard twin and pole out until it was almost pointing forward. Then I raised the mainsail, with a reef, and sailed for a time on a broad reach. Later back to twins.
Winds still off the starboard quarter.
2400
Cse – 260° – 270°
Wind picking up. Little Breeze is doing real well self-steering under twins with wind way off of the starboard quarter. Note: I was sleeping from 2000 until 0230. Made fantastic miles so I divided them up by putting what I thought appropriate on

WE'VE HIT THE TRADES!

Saturday's miles and the rest on Sunday's miles.
43.4 nautical miles daily run
717.2 total nautical miles traveled
(Made my minimum miles and I am on schedule.)

JOURNAL

I am really beginning to have a problem with my dreams while asleep at night. The dreams have become childlike nightmares. They are very real and vivid and I have a hard time recognizing when I am dreaming and when I am awake. The boat is so dark inside that when I open my eyes it still appears as though I am sleeping. My dreaming is most active in the morning between 4:00 a.m. and 7:30 a.m. It feels wonderful at the beginning, being among people, walking around with grass, trees, and buildings and with people talking to each other. But soon the dream takes a wicked turn and I'm in danger of being hurt or I watch someone else possibly being harmed. And when I awake I am glad to be here on my boat, in this reality and away from the terrifying helplessness.

Today was another typical day, as it has been for some time now. Overcast and calm in the morning, sunny and clear by late afternoon, a breeze picking up by three or four o'clock, with clouds congregating again by dusk. Oh, the twilight hours. A magnificent array of oranges, yellows, and reds mixing and blending together as the sun departs behind the low lying clouds and sinks slowly into the sea on the distant horizon. All this against a light blue sky as if it were a canvas backdrop to a magnificent painting.

CHAPTER TWELVE

I took advantage of a cool and calm morning to rearrange the locker and cabin areas. I emptied the forward locker, swabbed it out and then filled it with empty water containers, light dry goods, and packaged clothes to start lightening the load in the bow. My rearranging the cabin area might not have been for efficiency, comfort or convenience, but merely for a change of scenery.

After reading and dozing I made my first batch of *Little Breeze* biscuits to help with my bread supply for the up and coming week. I make flattened dough balls out of Bisquick and water then drop them into my little pot after first greasing the bottom with Pam vegetable oil and heating the pot as hot as I dare. They cook and brown just a bit and turn into something similar to a biscuit. With a little jam or honey on it, it's pretty good. I think I will make this a routine part of every weekend.

Nothing much else to say, I'm on my fourth book: (1) Wind Chime Legacy – A.W. Mykel, (2) Kidnapped – Robert Lewis Stevenson, (3) Moby Dick – Herman Melville, and (4) Voyage – Sterling Hayden. This last one is an amazing tale of dozens of characters in the late 1800s, all woven around several incredible voyages and seafaring tales. Another day—another mile.

TAPE

"Good evening to you ladies and gents. Time again for your after dinner oratory by the lone adventurer, explorer, captain and all around good guy, Michael Mann. Hey, I am still here. It's been a nice typical Saturday in the trades.

WE'VE HIT THE TRADES!

Evening—approximately twenty-five degrees north latitude, one hundred twenty-eight degrees west longitude. Whether that's good or bad is not the question right now. The question is how much longer is this going to take? I planned for forty days; thirty would have been a miracle. I have pretty much given up on that idea, seeing as how I am sixteen days out and have barely covered 700 miles, give or take a mile. I have now set my estimated time of arrival (ETA) date to fifty days, which would be about the end of July.

"Hoping all goes well. I may be in for some unpredictable weather. I have probably been in the eye of a high pressure system that moved a little farther south than usual. It's been two weeks of overcast, but as of late, I've had sunny weather. I could be in for a big blow real soon. I think I am prepared. I just hate getting wet, but at least the weather is comfortably warm.

"Right now the twins are up and the wind is from the northeast. *Little Breeze* is clipping along at three point two knots. Winds came out of the north for a while today, forcing me to reach. Other than having only logged 270 miles this week, everything is okay, going real well. Daily average miles have been forty-four point six miles. If the winds would blow like they are right now, I could really put in some miles. Hoping to have sailed 1,000 miles by next week.

"Sure wish I had taken the time to get a little more of a variety of canned goods and stocked up on batteries and smokes. Quitting smoking is a definite possibility whether I like it or not.

"Look at that sunset, great sight. Colors you would never believe. A photographer would be going wild on this trip.

CHAPTER TWELVE

In fact, I wish I had a 35mm camera. All I have is a little instamatic. The next picture I take is going to be either a fish I hope to catch on this line I have been towing the whole time, or of a ship that passes me. And I hope for the latter.

"Well, that is going to do it for tonight. See you again same time, same channel, same sea."

Sunday
June 27 – Day 17

LOG

0235
Wind still steady as she goes. It sure would be great if I could keep this pace up through tomorrow.
0822
Wind still steady out of the northeast.
Clouds obscure the sky. Swell 3 foot with
1 – 2 foot seas.
1237
25°34'N
128°24'W
I think I really screwed up today!
I messed around with the index error adjustment screw on the sextant because the sun was splitting down the middle. I turned the screw this way and that without any visual results. The sight I took put me over 60 miles west of my DR position. It will be impossible to calibrate again without a building or pole in the distance to sight it on.
2100

Large swell out of the west.
Winds dying out a bit. Made good miles today.
Hope for more of the same tomorrow.
2400
The breeze is warm and dry tonight.
Seas a little calmer.
Breeze steady northeast by east.
Watch error 23 seconds fast.
61 nautical miles daily run
(This is more like it. I knew I could travel miles like this with a steady breeze.)
778.2 total nautical miles traveled

JOURNAL

I can't say what exactly is the matter, but I feel real depressed today even though I've been making the good miles I've been hoping for. I guess it is because the sea is rough and confused. The skies have been overcast and steel-grey, all kind of reflecting the way I feel. Maybe I'm becoming lonely or maybe I am scared, but won't admit it. I guess it's best to say it and be done with it, rather than let it interfere with my thinking, which may in fact make matters worse. My mood is solemn.

I ate the last of my chocolate today. I would sleep for a week if I knew that I would keep sailing in the right direction. Patience Michael, you'll be there soon enough and you'll be sleeping and eating and drinking among your fellow man, you'll proudly pat yourself on the back, and will be planning your next adventure soon enough.

CHAPTER TWELVE

I can't be that far off the beaten path. Who knows, maybe ships have been passing me by day and night just beyond the horizon. Commercial ship traffic that travels much faster than my *Little Breeze* could be out of sight and over the horizon in only minutes.

Monday
June 28 – Day 18

LOG
0511
Wild night. Can't sleep. The relative humidity is causing extremely dry air and the wind keeps changing direction and strength. Swells keep rocking us so violently I'm afraid something is going to give. At least we are still moving.
0900
Cse – W
Swell 6 foot still from the northwest combined with a swell 1 – 2 foot from the east. Light breeze, overcast skies, might be starting to clear.
1300
Cse – Variable 255° – 270°
Winds are still light and have been out of the northwest. Took down one of the twins and am now on a broad reach.
Swells running from both east and northeast. Skies clear, except for some high wispy clouds.
1614 – 1648

WE'VE HIT THE TRADES!

Cse – Variable 190° – 255°
Wind back to northeast somewhat.
Main down, twins up. Been having scattered drizzles all afternoon.
Having problems with navigation; losing faith in myself. Have I been subtracting variation when I should have been adding 13° to my magnetic course to get true course? I don't know! Could sure use a fix from someone; otherwise I am guessing the rest of the way. The confounded wind is out of the north-northwest.
2100
Was heading west until becalmed, at least there isn't enough wind to fill the sail.
Sails down—drifting pretty much west.
35.9 nautical miles daily run
814.1 total nautical miles traveled

CHAPTER THIRTEEN

Ships That Pass in the Night

Tuesday
June 29 – Day 19

LOG
Still becalmed.
Another night camped out on a fathomless ocean.
There is a breeze out of the southwest.
How could that be? And if so, why for so long?
Give me strength.
Will fight for every bloody mile come morning.
0435
Winds west to northwest.
Small squall from northwest.
0920
25°40'N
130°32'W MPP
Cse – 265° – 270°
Wind still out of the north,
maybe it will come around to the east soon.
1445 –1733

CHAPTER THIRTEEN

Wind from north. Swell from northwest
3 – 5 foot with one foot chop.
The wind is churning the water
creating scattered whitecaps.
Large, billowy cotton balls of clouds
with dark bottoms and bright white tops,
otherwise hot.

1733
25°36'N
131°06'W
Cse – 270°

1900
Variable course 235° – 250°
Put in a reef in the main while I prepare dinner.

2031
Swell and winds still out of the north
10 – 15 knots, 3 – 5 foot, 1 – 2 foot chop.
Scattered whitecaps continue.

2235
Cse – 260°
Had to add a second reef,
doing 4.4 knots in the gusts.
Three-quarter moon out.
Clear tonight; the stars of this night sky
are too numerous and can't be counted.
Wind 15 knots gusting 20 knots.
Watch error 24 seconds fast.
65.3 nautical miles daily run
879.4 total nautical miles traveled

JOURNAL

I must say things around here sure jump around from bad to worse to better to worse again. Yesterday I woke up late; I hadn't slept so well, to find the swells still thrashing me about, but even worse was the wind changing around from the north. I figured once you're in the trades that was it. Well, it wasn't! So I was going to have to change the sails back to the fore and aft setup. I improvised by taking just one jib of the twins down, thinking that maybe easterlies would blow soon and in this condition I trudged along at a snail's pace with the sails giving a violent wallop now and then. I hate changing the rig around! It's not that it takes all that much time, but having to fold all these sails up again is tedious. Eventually, during the night or this morning, I took the twin sails down all together and stuffed them in a sail bag.

Yesterday was kind of a slow day all around. About the only thing I accomplished was finishing my fourth novel. It was really exciting until the end and like most epics it sort of left me flat.

TAPE

"Approximately a little over 800 miles from Los Angeles. For the past few days, we have been having easterly winds which I thought meant I was in the trades. Last night, the winds came up from the north. Had a small squall with a calm period just prior to it. Seas aren't so bad. Winds steady at ten knots. All sails are up with jib sheet controlling, self-steering. Approximate due west course.

CHAPTER THIRTEEN

Nothing else to report. All is about the same. My position right now is where I should have been this past Saturday (four days ago).

"I knew things were going to be long and arduous, dreary and boring, painstaking, depressing, beautiful, but I never should have underestimated time. Especially time alone! I am in the midst of a sea of solitude!

"I don't miss any inanimate material from the mainland really. I don't miss television, the phone or stereo. Maybe it is just the human element. I need to talk with somebody—*I really do*! That is why I keep talking on this blasted machine. I would love to see a ship. I would love to talk with somebody. I haven't used my radio; I am trying to conserve the battery. The power of communication is taken for granted.

"I know that things aren't that bad. I could have been soaking wet last night. *Little Breeze* couldn't be sailing any better. The boat is fantastic. It's been me, my choice of sails, setups, my sheeting arrangements, my self-steering, my navigation, my awareness of the environment and the ocean, how to handle it and how to project the boat through the sea. I guess I just didn't have the experience, but I am committed now. I am going to make it by God!

"I am going to make it clean. I am going to be in good spirits, I'll be happy and healthy when I get there. I am not going to be passed out and drifting along like a castaway without hope. I am going to be in total control of the situation. I am in total control of the situation right now.

"It's a mighty big world we live in. I wonder what this ocean looked like to the early explorers. A lot of people have navigated this sea without any idea of what they would find.

Oh to sail by just a star and the sun and moon alone. At least I am not trying to sail around Cape Horn in this thing. Maybe someday I will—just kidding!

"You'll never believe it—I just spotted my first freighter since I left the coast! I don't know if that is good or not, but it is sure a welcome sight to see. It is heading north-northeast approximately five miles off my starboard, abaft the beam.

"I am on a westerly heading. Wow, it is a loaded freighter. I must be going in the right direction. *YA...HOOO!* Now I am going to have to keep watch tonight. That sucker is big. I didn't even see him. I was in my cabin reading and he sailed right past me. I tried to make contact on channel 16 VHF, but no response. Tried a few other channels, but still no response. I cannot describe what a beautiful sight that freighter was. I am confident that I'm where I am supposed to be. I'll bet that baby is heading to Los Angeles! I could have surely used an updated position from him. It was clear I was not going to have any human conversation last night.

"It has been about sixteen days since I have seen any living thing except for some terns, an albatross, and those pilot whales I saw a while back. Man, oh man—I wonder what this night has in store! I am going to leave the rest of this tape open to give an up-to-the-minute report."

Wednesday
June 30 – Day 20

LOG
0342
255°

CHAPTER THIRTEEN

Wind increasing.
Don't know if I can keep jib up much longer.
Small rain squall.
0630
25°32'N
131°55'W
Winds still about the same. One reef.
Skies clearing. Seas turbulent.
1045
Tried taking sight. Not even close.
1452
25°28'N
132°22'W
Cse – 255°
Have set twins. Tried my hand at reefing them.
Looks pretty shabby. Winds picking up, the waves are broken with foaming white crests.
1942
Cse – 210° – 215° magnetic
Seas confused. Swells mounting,
forming huge valleys. Twins looking good,
except that they only steer downwind.
When the wind veers, so does the course.
2300
Running bare pole, southwest wind
20 – 25 knots, gusting 30 knots
east-northeast.
White capping swells.
Six-foot short period swells from east-northeast with long period swells from the north.

Took down sails—Warp Out!
76.4 nautical miles daily run
955.8 total nautical miles traveled

JOURNAL

And so ends the month of June 1982. The past three days have brought good winds, fair seas, and a small rain squall for the past two nights. Didn't sleep much last night; couldn't stop thinking about ships.

Today makes my twentieth day out from Huntington Harbor. I have had good wind and seas. I have been through heavy weather. I've been becalmed and adrift, and lost and alone. My hope was reinforced yesterday with the sighting of a ship after nineteen days. At the moment, although battered by swells, I am making good progress.

The skies have been mostly clear and the weather warm.

I have had no problems with *Little Breeze* except for some mysterious seepage into the cabin lockers and self-steering in ultra-light wind. Have spent 90 percent of my time in the cabin, cleaning, reading, and just sitting, and about 10 percent outside either changing sails, setting up the steering, adjusting it, or steering by hand when the wind was too light.

Have been eating regularly. Provisions are still intact. I am just recently experiencing pain in my neck, lower back and joints. Sleeping hasn't been good lately. Perhaps my lack of fiber rich foods and lack of exercise are taking a toll on me. Inside the confines of my cabin I tend to lie in the same position as I read and I do a lot of that.

CHAPTER THIRTEEN

All in all things are going as planned. It is just that I could never plan or practice being alone for fifty to sixty days.

As I have said, I have been eating regularly. My favorite vegetables have been the zucchini, green beans, and corn, in that order. The lima beans I can't stand! My most enjoyable main meal is Dinty Moore. Other combinations of concoctions I've contrived are Rice-a-Roni with chunks of ham, a cup full of Minute Rice with an egg, Cream of Chicken or Mushroom soup with rice thrown in at the end, mashed potatoes with melted Velveeta cheese or margarine, and finally Top-Ramen with any number of things mixed in is always good. I wish I had brought more spaghetti type dinners.

My cans of fruit cocktail, pears and peaches are good anytime. Open the can, suck the juice out, eat the rest and toss the cans over the side knowing they will eventually deteriorate in the sea.

For breakfast it is mainly oatmeal one day, eggs the next, a biscuit with jam or honey, and a cup of tea or hot coffee.

Coffee, tea, Tang and hot chocolate are drinks I make with water. Or there is pineapple, apple, or grapefruit juice. As it turns out Hansen papaya and pear nectars are not good warm. To try and cool those down I would lash six packs to the transom and drag them through the cold ocean water. But now the Pacific Ocean temperature is too warm so I will save those drinks for the islands.

Raisins, peanuts and nuts are good to munch in-between meals and I wish I had more. As are M&Ms and brownies, which I just ran out of.

Food has been the main thing I look forward to on a day to day basis. My morning, noon and night ritual is to boil hot water and put it in the thermos for later. Pick out a can, box or packet for a meal. Mix and or cook up the dish. Make coffee, tea or hot chocolate, then sit back and enjoy the panoramic view.

I am a little disappointed on the way I've been letting *Little Breeze* deteriorate into a pig's sty. She's so cluttered all of a sudden. I guess that's because I am without a convenient place to stash dirty clothes. I will make an effort to correct the situation.

I hope I find a warm reception in the islands. I could sure use a little help, like a dock with a hose and a shower that I can use for a few days while I unload this barge, dump the trash, wash some clothes, and wash me and my boat down. I am becoming what you might call potent and I am sure if the boats passing me don't see me, they smell me when they get down wind.

I'm just going to close with a little bad news. I think I've misaligned my sextant for good. It looks like I will be using Dead Reckoning for the remainder of this voyage!

TAPE

"Some 900 miles out of Los Angeles. It seems only appropriate that I end the month on the first side of the first tape. Twenty days I've been at sea. No sign of any ships during the night, although I was up quite often. I am not only worried about ships, but also this weather. It has been what I asked for, active—very active.

CHAPTER THIRTEEN

"Getting a northeast wind but I sure would hate to put up my twins right now. There is my friend the frigate bird. Good to see him; the birds have been a welcome sight. I guess it's a form of entertainment for me in my solitude.

"Sun is rising in the east. Scattered clouds. Seas wild, no whitecaps, but rougher than I ever imagined. Steering a westerly course. Not much else to say. Will write a summary of the trip's events so far and then go over my stores when the weather calms down. Been making fantastic miles the past couple days. The freighter seen yesterday was sure an inspirational boost to my mental state. New batteries in tape recorder.

"*Little Breeze* is fairing really well. I can't believe that sheets of Dacron and this rigging can move her along like this. I have started the book *Hawaii* by James Michener. He describes the creation of an island; molten basaltic rock forming layers upon layers through millions and millions of years. The very first people to take refuge on that island planted their tribal culture there and it lasted until the white man came in to westernize everything. I will see the results of our intrusion.

"I said before that I did not have any desire for commercial television, radio and newspaper, but lately I have been starting to dream TV—like *Mash* episodes. It must be the remnants of pre-programmed years during childhood and as an adult growing up in the age of television entertainment. If I were to have children now, I would start developing them more intellectually and physically, rather than letting them sit around and watch hours of television every day like I used to do.

"Well, June is over. June has always been my favorite month. My last day at school was June 11, 1980, when I graduated from Orange Coast College, after a year at Humboldt State, and a quarter at Peninsula College, Washington. My year at Orange Coast was my favorite year at school. Before then, I would just try to slide through, but my last year at Orange Coast really meant something to me. I had a goal to be a marine technician. I worked hard, made good grades and was recognized and acknowledged by my peers and teachers. I felt really good about myself and my work. Those days are gone.

"I guess when you get past the age of twenty, unless you have a really good goal at school, you should begin to think more of an occupation and trade, rather than going to school every day. I hope to go back to school someday, I really enjoyed it!

"It will be July tomorrow. Four days until the fourth, Independence Day. I remember quite a few parties on Independence Day, especially on Catalina Island. Catalina—that's another long story. I will be celebrating my own little Independence Day out here. I am independent out here to a point. I hope my mom hasn't had a fire in her house because I left an M-80 firecracker on top of the shelf in my room and a few sky rockets in the garage. Should have brought them with me.

"Hopefully, by the fourth I will have put in a 1,000 miles. Close to halfway, but I zigged when I should have zagged back there. My navigation isn't all that it's cracked up to be. Who knows, maybe I am right on. Fifty days isn't really that long. I was hoping to make great time. Thirty days does not

CHAPTER THIRTEEN

sound unreasonable if I could do seventy miles a day and head right there. I would sure like to hail a big freighter and say, 'Hey buddy—got a road map?'

"I am being hit right now by a storm like the one I met when I was off San Clemente, only *BIGGER*. Took down twins for fear that they would have been most assuredly blown out. Right now I am locked in, hanging on, warp is out. The swell is definitely from the northeast, pushing me southwest, which is fine and dandy. These swells are really big. Getting hit by long period, very large swell from the north which adds to the trials and tribulations. Here, have a listen (put microphone outside into the howling wind). See what I mean. Anyway, if I don't get run over by any monster ships I just might make it through this. Hopefully in one piece. Man, what an impressive ocean!

"It figures that this would be the culmination of the past few nights. Not sure if I have a gale or not. It's probably just a squall. I guess one positive thing is that I put in the most miles today—seventy miles, which is good. Yesterday, I put in sixty miles, which makes it about 130 miles in two days. Not bad."

Thursday
July 1 – Day 21

LOG
0830
Running bare pole SW.
One stormy night! Everything still the same.
1000

Cse – 210° – 240°
Put up twins with a reef.
Swell still 4 to 5 feet.
Wind east by northeast.
1250
Turned the bottom of the sumlog back to 000.0, I finally hit a 1,000 miles.
On the face of the VDO are two digital readouts, one for total miles and one for running miles which can be set back to zero (similar to a car odometer).
1618
25°08'N
133°35'W
Cse – 240°
Approximately 25 more days to cover 1,200 miles at 48 miles a day. Twins still doing well.
Wind now 20 knots. Seas somewhat calmer. Skies clearer.
2000
Seas getting a little rougher. Hope not like last night. Could ride happily through the night in these conditions. (Guess the following swell could add at least one knot.)
2340
Light winds tonight until midnight, then picking up. Seas calm for now.
51.4 nautical miles daily run
1,007 total nautical miles traveled

CHAPTER THIRTEEN

TAPE

"It is a little too rough to write, so I am recording today's journal. As you can tell I made it through the storm. It was one of the most intense nights of the voyage. It was awesome and frightening at the same time. *Little Breeze* has been reaffirmed as stable and sea worthy. Right now we are making pretty good time with reefed twins. I am bone-tired, almost to the point of exhaustion! The bird is back. Doesn't look like a seagull; maybe it's an albatross.

"There I was a 1,000 miles from anywhere, alone in a 15-foot boat, warped out, survival conditions. To think about it, there would be no way for me to put out in my raft, because if it comes to that, it means the boat is lost and I would be lost. The odds of recovery, particularly at night or on high seas are pretty slim. So I have to do everything in my power to keep this boat floating, which so far has not been a chore. I thought for sure the rig was going to blow down last night. The rattle and monotonous hum were deafening. I have been locked down in my cabin as the swells have tossed my boat from left to right, rolling constantly. Finally, an enormous wave almost knocked *Little Breeze* on her side. If there had been repeated hits from that direction I may have been broached, which would have been an extremely dangerous situation out here by myself. I did everything I could to try to sleep but no luck! Put out my strobe mast head light and emergency radar reflector praying that no one would hit me, so I could just get some sleep.

"Things didn't start calming down until nine o'clock this morning when I was finally able to hoist the sail. When the VDO sumlog clicked over to 1,000 miles at noon I came to the realization—I'm still not halfway yet! Like I said before, I may have made some decisions near the start, which may have added one hundred miles to my trip. That will be hind sight when I reach the islands. Sure would like to get a fix to confirm my current position. Here it is July and it will probably be August by the time I arrive there—I hope not!"

Friday
July 2 – Day 22

LOG
0430
Cse – Variable 240° – 260°
0844
24°50'N
134°29'W
Cse – Variable 260° – 280°
Reefed twins still up and still steering
(my back hurts and I am extremely sleep deprived).
1041
Put up full twins. Swells dying and screwy.
1200
Wind picking up.
1400
Steering all over.
Swells from east and north.
1700
Things are a little calmer now;
winds and seas are fair.
1800
24°39'N

CHAPTER THIRTEEN

135°04'W MPP
Cse – 240°
Wind bearing north barely northeast and dying.
Forced to sail south if I want to keep twins up.
Come around wind!
2000
Winds out of the north.
Had to change to the fore and aft rig.
Twins down, broad reach.
Please stay this way for the night!
2200
Cse – 290°
Wind came back around from the east—oh no!
So I'll head a little north tonight.
2330
Cse – 280° magnetic
Wind now east-northeast.
Riding a little north but swinging 260° – 290°
76 nautical miles daily run
1083 total nautical miles traveled

JOURNAL

Stayed up most of the night keeping the boat from jibing. Had some rain again early morning. Wind fifteen knots northeast. Swells northeast.

The mighty sea has seen fit to give me a break from the relentless pounding it gave me the past three days. The nights are by far the worst, the way the sea changes its composure, from wild and aggressive to calm and subtle. I'm fascinated and at times terrified by its immensity. That the oceans can exist within their boundaries and not flood our low-lying coastal areas is amazing. As far as allowing ships and other such vessels to venture over its mass, I hope that I, in my *Little Breeze*, am allowed to pass.

In my opinion, the sea holds that secret of life that we humans have been in search of since the beginning of recorded time. Down in its depths, among the muck and darkness, life exists that has survived since the beginning of time, something for which there is no time, just a state of being. When one looks out over the face of an open body of ocean, one may only see a desolate, hostile exterior. If only we could penetrate into its depths, as I have done while scuba diving, then we could experience the serene tranquil environment that exists there altogether devoid of human designs. Feel the water surrounding you and you will feel a peace that you have not felt since leaving your mother's womb. For the sea will be our salvation in the future if we keep her well and free from poisons and waste. The sea will help feed, power, and entertain us and maybe even house us in the conflicting years to come.

Our troubles on land are our own and should not overflow into the sea in disputes over who owns the sea. No one owns the sea—the sea is. It exists. And it will never be anyone's, although we already lease the rights to mine the minerals within continental jurisdictions. As our technology progresses, we will seek deeper and farther out until a line will have to be drawn and I foresee fighting over that which belongs to all people.

As for myself, I am hot, hungry, tired, sore, bored, lonely

CHAPTER THIRTEEN

and scared. That about says it all. Twenty-two days since I left comfortable Orange County, with its In-n-Out Burger restaurants, movie theatres, bathrooms, and showers.

I wonder what the family is doing. I wonder if they've given up on me, I did tell them it could take as long as forty days. I wonder if I truly have a friend in this world. What is a friend? Is there land or am I destined to eternally drift among these waves? Will I run out of food and water after days of hallucinations? I wonder.

Every day appears the same but I guess there is a difference. It is becoming hard to tell and that is what scares me. Another day, another sixty miles covered. I keep going over and over the figures in my head—controlling myself, telling myself this, soon, another week and you'll be close. Two weeks and maybe you'll see a ship. Three weeks and maybe you'll see land. Four weeks and maybe you'll go mad. I tell you mad—mad!

I'm supposed to be contemplating my career—my future. How can I when I don't see any light?

I hope Hawaii is as beautiful as I read about in Michener's terrific novel. I hope I am welcomed.

TAPE

"I guess I've been in a storm for three days now. Too turbulent to continue writing, so here I am on tape again. Making good time, but lately winds are slack and I took the reef out of my twins. The motion of the ocean is not cooperating. I am getting really confused; the seas appear to be coming from all directions and we are getting hit by large sets of northerly swells every half hour. No wind, just heavy drizzle. Can't get the boat to self-steer correctly. I was with it all night for the past two nights. I could really use some sleep, but things are so brutal out that I can't—no way. The only things I have been able to eat today have been a can of peaches earlier and just now some nuts, coffee and oatmeal. My muscles are sore beyond belief and I am exhausted. I need some calm seas and a light breeze to get some sleep or to clean the boat out. I hope this weather doesn't last too much longer. The weather is clear in the distance but where I am is miserable.

"Last night I spotted what I think was a masthead light in the distance heading southwest off my starboard. From 4:30 to 5:30 a.m. I watched it track across and pass me, and like a ghost ship, fade into the horizon. It moved past slowly, leaving me alone once again. I wonder if they were having cocktails last night while I was swinging and swaying and sweating it out. Well I need to tend to *Little Breeze*. Maybe another recording later.

"I wonder if I actually thought I was going to do this for fun. So far this has been one of the most grueling challenges and I am sore and dog-tired. I am caked with salt and I am still just about halfway. This *is* the mighty Pacific.

"I am pretty sure I am in the trades, but where exactly, I don't know. This is a challenge alright. But it all looks the same. The only thing I notice is the sun and the moon. I think I've been staying on the same latitude covering great longitudinal distances. Approximate twenty-four degrees, fifteen minutes north, one hundred thirty-four degrees, fifty minutes west. Now that I covered 1,007 miles, that means I have 1,200 miles to go.

"If I could only get a fix from someone. I have dreams where a boat pulls up and I ask, 'Hey where am I?' Too tired to do much now, like clean *Little Breeze*, clean myself, cook or sail. Sailing is the only thing I break my back to do. Keep me moving. Keep those miles accumulating. It's frustrating when the sea is so rough and I don't have any wind at all. With the wind I can maintain forward momentum and glide through it. When I am sitting like a rock, the boat swings left and right—up and down. The poles crash back and forth, and *Little Breeze* zigzags, twirls and jibes. It is an incredible sight though, mounds and mounds of water meeting clouds in the sky. I wonder how far my visible horizon is. I climb up on top of my cabin and scan 360 degrees, no luck except for a few days back when I spotted that freighter—it seems like a year ago now. That freighter passed by quickly. It means I could be down in the cabin reading for an hour and a ship could pass by and I wouldn't even know it. However, reading is the only thing keeping me going right now."

Saturday
July 3 – Day 23

LOG

0140
Bare poling heading southwest.
Wind is up out of the northeast.
Had to take down sails, warp out.
Not as intense as the night before.
Last night rain, twins up with reef

and it took a long time to set sail.
1200
Cse – 230°
New sight for this zone (135° west central meridian)
put me at 24°39'N
Still trying to use my sextant.
1607
24°39'N
136°17'W Rfx
Cse – Variable 230° – 240°
Winds picking up after a relatively calm day.
Whitecaps. Winds steady out of the east-northeast.
Easterly swell,
winds look to be veering north again.
1900
Winds shifting to north again.
I guess I will let it ride.
Around 0100 wind will likely start to swing back.
2300
All's well.
59.0 nautical miles daily run
1142 total nautical miles traveled

JOURNAL

Just one short entry for today. All is going well. I had myself a small case of jock itch. So I really washed and powdered myself. I cannot have something like that getting out of hand. Gerry Spiess reported he had a case the whole way across the Atlantic. My scalp and beard are flaking so

CHAPTER THIRTEEN

badly that it looks like snow. In my left ear there is a little lump that is starting to hurt. I washed it with some alcohol; I hope it is not serious.

Weather has been warm day and night. It has rained on and off the past five days. Easterly winds are still blowing. Once in a while they will swing to the north, annoying me, as then I have to decide whether to switch rigs, and when I do it seems that after only a few hours, just when I am getting comfortable, the wind switches back.

Made good time last week averaging, fifty-eight point four miles a day. Nothing else new. Aloha.

TAPE

"Unbelievable! I've sighted my first sailboat. As I glanced around the horizon, like I always do, around 7:30 p.m. (PDST), I unmistakably saw an orange and white spinnaker flying off my port beam. This is so exciting! Right there off my port is a sailboat with a spinnaker flying. She's a good ten miles out. She's cruising, but I am keeping up. Look at that. I'll be! It is such a pretty sight to see another boat out here. Swells are getting big now. Twelve feet easily, but when they crest some are sixteen feet.

"Today has been a good day. Haven't seen any squalls. But I hate to speak too soon. I had my twins up with a reef all day. Should have had them up full, but I am feeling rather lazy these days. I am satisfied with four knots. I am going to keep my eyes on that sail until it is dark. I tried to contact them on VHF but no response, guess people don't care to leave their radios on out here. I wonder if they even see me; I am almost buried in these swells. I must be doing something right. When the chips are down it takes something like that to build up your spirits again. Those guys are moving along pretty good. It looks like we are on a parallel course. I am heading about 220 degrees magnetic west. If they see me, I wonder if they think I am real or not. God I wish they would respond to the radio. I am sure they could pick me up. I don't think they can self-steer with a spinnaker up. It looks like they also have their main up. I can see the upper part of the rigging, but I can't see the boat. If only we could get closer. It is 7:45 and I still have them in sight. What more entertainment could you ask for on a Saturday night? A good breeze behind you, the sun going down on one side and watching a sail pass by on the other.

"Eight forty-four p.m. and like the sun, my fellow sailors are sinking into the horizon. I can just make out the top of their sails now. As I watch them travel west into the horizon I'm disappointed that I couldn't find out who they were and share a few words—maybe next time. The full moon is already up off to port, pretty high in the sky. Let's just keep it sailing tonight boys, alright?"

CHAPTER FOURTEEN

Halfway
My Point of No Return

Sunday
July 4 – Day 24

LOG

0320
Cse – 220° – 240°
Rain – shook reef out of twins.

0730
Woke up early, seas are fair to good.
Twins are up full. Wind maybe 15 knots
and we are powering through the waves.

1130
Winds constant 12 knots east by
east-northeast. 2-foot seas over a 6-foot swell.
Cloudy, maybe clearing later on.
WE – 27 seconds fast.

1404
C – 250°
Cloud covered sun, no sight today.

1537

CHAPTER FOURTEEN

Bare pole – course still 250 degrees magnetic.
Winds gusting approximately 30 knots,
sails down, no warp out yet.
Bare pole traveling 2 knots from east to west.
1900
24°05'N
137°57'W
Bare pole heading 230° – 250° magnetic.
Winds still too strong to hoist sail.
Now I have too much wind!
At least the sea is not too angry.
Still no warp out.
2100
Winds 25 knots gusting 35 knots east by northeast,
seas 2 – 4 feet, breaking swell
6 – 8 – 10 feet from the northeast.
No warp. Little Breeze riding rather well.
There are short and long period swells.
2300
Winds stronger. Warp out.
71.6 nautical miles daily run
1213.6 total nautical miles traveled

JOURNAL

Independence Day—I have been looking forward to this day because it is the first, and probably only, national holiday I will spend in the middle of the Pacific. It marks what I am confident is my halfway point. It was a day I set aside to look forward to when I first set out. Well, I'm still here and

HALFWAY MY POINT OF NO RETURN

I guess I'm still somewhat on schedule. This appears to be my physical and emotional point of no return! To return to the mainland at this juncture I would be beating into heavy weather and forced to travel hundreds of miles north before heading east.

My sextant still plays tricks on me. Most of the time I'm close (within twenty miles), sometimes right on (within five miles), but other times I cannot even get the sights to calculate out. I cannot wait to get to land to see how far out of alignment the sextant really is.

I have thought about writing letters to the folks but I'm too lazy and it looks like my chances of getting someone to pick them up out here are poor. Even if someone could get close enough, it would just be too rough to pass the package. I sure hope all is well at home and they haven't called out the Coast Guard—yet!

Now it is time to think about dinner. I don't know; I am beginning to lose my appetite for the food I've brought.

Ah, what I would give for a nice thick steak, medium rare, smothered in onions, fresh mashed potatoes with a large glob of butter, fresh celery sticks, cauliflower, carrots, a nice big salad with blue cheese dressing, applesauce, an ice cold glass of milk, later some ice cream and finally, after all that, some expensive ice cold imported beer. I have just ruined my dinner of Dinty Moore Beef Stew!

I sense that everyone is thinking about me and it is their hope that gives me the strength to persevere when I feel sad and lonely and so very far away.

I will kiss each and every one when I see them again.

Love you all—Michael

CHAPTER FOURTEEN

TAPE

"Independence Day! Hurray, hurray, hurray, and all that good stuff. For me it is just another day at sea. I would just like to take this time to describe a few of the techniques I have been able to accomplish with the boat, as far as self-steering in the different points of sail. The following is my interpretation and adaptation of self-steering techniques described in John Leetcher's book *Self-Steering*.

"First: Beating to windward and close reaching method. You use 'main sheet control method', whereby the control line is bent onto the main sheet (in my case onto the boom), and then brought through a block tied to the coaming on the windward side and then tied to the tiller. The leeward side of the tiller is stabilized by a bungee. Depending on the strength of the wind, and the elasticity of the bungee (in my case surgical tubing), the bungee can be cinched up to be stiff or slacked off to be lax. This technique can give satisfactory steering ten to twenty degrees on either side of your desired heading to windward depending on wind and swell variability and intensity. Winds and swells being constant, you then can trim your sails to achieve the desired course. Then adjust the control sheet so that the tiller is center or a little to leeward by tightening the bungee so the tiller has the ability to pull leeward or stretching slightly taunt when the wind causes the main sheet to pull. If wind and swells are not constant then the boat will sway or yawl. This will slow you down and make sailing uncomfortable.

"Second: Beam and broad reaching method. When broad reaching, the main sheet is unable to provide the proper tiller control. I have been able to take the jib sheet through a block on the leeward side, then through a block on the weather side and then to the tiller. The bungee, again attached on the leeward side, is adjusted in the previously mentioned manner. In this way I have been able to accomplish satisfactory steering in different wind intensities and sea conditions with the wind on the beam. When the wind becomes too strong the storm jib needs to be set. With a storm jib, a pulley system is needed to provide the small jib with the torque needed to influence the tiller. Note: when the wind picks up and I have to reef, I don't have to readjust the self-steering.

"Third: Twin jibs running method. The wind at this point is dead astern or slightly off to one quarter or another. The twins are raised for running. The sails can be adjusted slightly forward or back depending on wind intensity. Raising the twins is not the most graceful thing to watch. But once up, the sheets are run back through blocks on coamings on their respective sides and tied to the tiller. The twins are able to maintain steerage within ten degrees on either side of desired heading depending on wind and swell strength and variability. This is how I have been sailing in the trades.

"When the wind becomes too intense, I can reef my twins. It is a hard job to slack the halyard, run forward, tighten the down haul, reef, and then run back and set sail again without having the sails flail. With the reef I am able to take a considerable amount of wind. With the full twins I am able to take wind off the quarter a bit more than with them reefed. With the swell coming in from the stern, *Little Breeze* rides like a rollercoaster. With the swell coming from any other direction she tends to swing about. But the self-steering will bring her back. To add support to the mast while running down wind I also rig the running backstays to the cleats on the port and starboard corners of the transom.

"I have only hand-steered when the wind is ultra-light—insufficient to fill the sails. I have had problems when I slept while the wind changed direction. The self-steering sailed to the 'apparent wind' not a true course, and so the course changed when the wind changed and I woke up to find *Little Breeze* sailing peacefully along, but on a different heading than when I went to sleep. Interesting to note that, except for my having to go to the bow to change jibs, I can operate *Little Breeze* through the hatch while standing in my cabin area. Reefing, tiller adjustment, raising and lowering of sail can all be reached and accomplished while standing in the cabin. That is my technical report number one—thank you.

"Well it did not turn out to be the tranquil, peace-loving Fourth of July I had envisioned. We started out good, had great miles going with full twins and cooperative winds. But all good things must come to an end and the winds are now determined to blow quite a bit harder, too hard even for a reef. Not entirely because of the winds but also because the surface conditions are so wild my self-steering would be pitiful. We are getting blown a good two knots in a westerly direction; I might as well ride it out for a while. No warp yet but if things get too rough I might do that. Right now skies are partly cloudy with a towering, gnarly wall of clouds approximately fifty miles to the south. Above me puffy cumulus scattered clouds with defined edges. White capped seas three to four feet, swells seven to ten feet. I saw a couple swells that led me to believe I would have to start bailing, but for some reason *Little Breeze* just gently descended down the waves. I feel like I am in a kayak on a huge river. Smaller boats just tend to ride up one side and down the other side of large swells and are not as prone to pounding as larger vessels.

"It's the Fourth of July and this weather isn't going to deter me from having a good time. I will sit and read and watch the sun go down, have a Coke and a cigarette, almost my last one. I shouldn't kid around like that. Sure would be nice to have another boat sighting to keep me on my toes. Hanging on here; you could say it is kind of volatile. I have sixty miles covered so far. I could have easily had a ninety mile day. I was doing four and a half knots since three o'clock this morning. If the gusts would stop, I could raise reefed twins. So that is it for now, unless I spot a freighter or something exciting like that. Twenty-four days out of Los Angeles, over 1,200 miles covered. ETA, Honolulu approximately the twenty-fifth of July. This is Mike Mann and the *Little Breeze* over and out."

July 5
Monday – Day 25

LOG
0200
Cse – 240° magnetic
Wind still strong, seas calmer,
pulled in warp, put up twins with reef
and have been sailing comfortably since.
0630

CHAPTER FOURTEEN

Cse – 230° – 240° magnetic
Seas calm, swell 4 – 6 feet,
wind 12 – 15 knots east by northeast.
0800
23°56'N
138°32'W
Large rolling swells. Had some more drizzle.
Sky is clearing.
0930
23°56'N
138°36'W
Cse – 220° – 250° magnetic
Winds coming around from north to northeast
forcing us to sail south to southwest.
I hope it comes back around.
1200
Cse – 220° magnetic
Full twins, wind strong, sea confused,
being rocked wildly back and forth.
1420
Averaging 230°
Some rain,
noon sight put me 20 miles south of DR position.
1600
Cse – variable 245° – 260°
Winds came back up like yesterday
and put reef in twins.
1826
23°39'N
139°07'W

Getting thrown about a bit,
but Little Breeze is holding her own.
2130
Until now course 230° – 250° magnetic
Sails still up—weather stable—full moon tonight.
Wind howling, I am afraid to take down sail.
Will keep on for an hour or two longer.
Wind warm but dry. Seas are fair.
80.8 nautical miles daily run
1294.4 total nautical miles traveled

TAPE

"It is interesting the way I surf down the face of the waves approaching from astern until they pass under me and then I get stopped dead in my tracks. I have pushed the boat today. I still have the twins up with a reef. Have had showers on and off for a week now, mostly at night. They last only twenty to thirty minutes. In the mornings I have been finding dead baby flying fish that have launched themselves onto my decks. If enough flying fish would get caught in my cockpit I would try eating them. I just watched a pair take flight across the waves only minutes ago. I am getting tired of the old canned goods. Winds are twenty knots gusting thirty knots. Skies are clear above, with a haze and possible showers in the distance.

"Had a real good morning. Cleaned up a bit in the cabin, then I stripped down in the cockpit and gave myself a thorough wash down. Remained there naked, lazily reclined against the cabin reading the novel *Hawaii*. Very interesting,

CHAPTER FOURTEEN

the racial and social development of the islands that I am about to see. It is a big book so I have to skip around and read things like the *War of the Worlds* and *Of Mice and Men*.

"If it were not for the seas I could probably take out the reefs. I am going to do eighty miles today if it kills me. Well, let's not say that. I have sixty miles so far. In the big pushes I do five knots, but then I drop down to two knots. Nothing else new to report, I am just counting down the days. Days and weeks have slipped by and things are getting a bit mundane. I'm burnt out. The motion is quite something. I remember when I couldn't stand pond-like seas—now I would give anything for it to calm down, but at least leave us some wind. The winds are from the northeast, forcing me a little farther south than I would like to go with Hawaii still another 800 miles away. I thought the winds would be more prevalent from the east at this latitude. Who knows, I might be farther north than I think. I have tried to do noon sights, but they put me either twenty miles north or south of my DR latitude.

"I have decided to just use running fixes and if they are close to my DR, I go with that. I guess by just sheer practice being up almost twenty-four hours a day taking in sails, letting out sails and changing the rig over and over, I am becoming quite proficient at it.

"There are lots of things I might put on the rig if I were to do this again. I might make another technical report about any changes in preparation for my next trip. I just want to make the best possible speed. I want to get from 140 degrees west to 150 degrees west in less than ten days. If I could do that I'd be sitting pretty.

"I am twenty-five days out of Los Angeles. Lately I've been doing sixty and seventy mile days. I am impressed with *Little Breeze's* stability. I remember back in California the winds would be gusting like this and she would be over on her rails. But now I'm going down wind and I have the weight of the added gear. I do get knocked around a bit. Some rolling from side to side, but she comes right back up. I have only taken one wave into the cockpit. I have had several poundings, like someone beating the hull with a sledge hammer. I am getting back pressure on my bilge pump, forcing the handle back and forth. The water is splashing through my cockpit drain plugs. It sure would be nice to make contact with another boat. Boy have I got a lot to say. I feel sorry for the first person I meet; I will talk their ears off."

Tuesday
July 6 – Day 26

LOG
0830
Position
23°29'N
140°04'W
Cse – 210° – 225° magnetic
Was real tired last night. I awoke at 0245,
0500 and 0630. As far as I can remember each
time the compass read 255 degrees to 270 degrees.
I just couldn't seem to wake up.
Right now it is raining.
Swells were up all night.

CHAPTER FOURTEEN

*Long period of 6 – 8 foot swells
out of the northeast.*
1404
Cse – 260° – 270° magnetic
Wind steady out of the east 7 – 12 knots.
Patchy scattered showers.
1600
Encountered 12-foot swells.
Three to four in a set every five minutes.
Decided to keep reefs in twin today.
1900
Cse – 260° magnetic
Winds actually decreasing.
Seas a little calmer.
2145
Twins still reefed.
Wind northeast backing north 15 knots.
Swells east 6 – 8 feet with an occasional monster.
Clouds are rolling in.
78 nautical miles daily run
1372.4 total nautical miles traveled

JOURNAL

It has always been a dream of mine to venture out into the isolated areas of the oceans in the hope of finding great herds of marine mammals, wondrous schools of fish and other creatures that neither I nor anyone else has encountered. Well in all these respects, I am a little disappointed. The creatures I have seen so far were familiar, few and close to the mainland. However, I have been surprised by the birds.

Every day I have seen marine birds gliding across the tops of waves and sliding through the troughs in search of food. I've seen four types of birds. Their types are best distinguished by their tails: forked, pintail or truncated. The fourth bird, I am sure was an albatross, but it wasn't as big as I thought it would be. I believe that from here on out the winds should be steady out of the east. I have been making sixty to seventy miles a day for a week now. With these winds and fair seas, I should sight land within twenty days.

These tropical latitudes are quite pleasant. There are warm winds during the day and night and the water is a considerably vivid blue and inviting. I can't wait to see the silhouette of the islands!

TAPE

"After a very speedy night with reefed twins I managed to make my first eighty mile day, eighty-one point eight miles to be exact. Things have been going really well. The twins have been up for approximately forty-eight hours. Because I am so close in latitude to the sun's declination, or the sun's latitude, I am going to attempt to take 'a high altitude sight or arc of position sight'. This should be possible within the next half hour. I have read about this sight reduction technique, but have never performed one.

"Technical report number two: Pertaining to twin jibs, self-steering. As far as the twins are concerned I have found that they perform more efficiently when set to billow a bit forward. Properly set they are able to steer in sizable amounts of wind and waves. I have been happy on that account because the winds last night had to be thirty knots, the whole time I was hoping that the rig would hold together.

"One of the added modifications to *Little Breeze* was to add two 'running backstays.' The cable length end was bolted one third of the way below the masthead, while the four-foot rope tails were attached to the other. I could tie off the rope tails to the port and starboard cleats on the transom, giving the mast added support with heavy winds from behind. The running backstays help to support the permanent backstays when the twin headsails are up.

"During the night I had a frightening nightmare about losing my mast with my sails ripping away, but thank goodness, when I woke up and looked, everything was still hanging in there.

"Each day I press the ability of my sails and rig. It now appears to me that I am farther north than I had imagined. This is alright with me because I've been worried about the opposite, being too far south. If I allow myself to get too far south I could miss the islands and may never be able to sail back north to windward. Today the sun's declination is twenty-two degrees, forty-nine minutes north while I calculate my latitude as being close to twenty-three degrees, thirty minutes north.

"Except for some very large swells, three to four in a set, everything is real nice. Crystal clear skies, sunny and hot. I almost got knocked down by a random rogue swell. Self-steering appears to be able to compensate so far. It is amazing to be on top of these swells; I can see for miles and then down between ridges of waves in the troughs, I am visually limited to about twenty feet around me.

"It occurs to me I have traveled through two time zones and am approaching a third. I have stayed on Pacific Daylight Savings Time (PDST) and it is three o'clock back in sunny southern California but is only noon here at around the 135 degree west time meridian. At 142 ½ degrees west, I will be entering my third and final time zone. This will put me another hour earlier than PDST. I was wondering why the sun stayed up until 10:30 last night. Since this is my first offshore navigating experience I have found that I still have a lot to learn about the art of navigation! This I'll study more when I get the chance. But in the meantime I will keep trying to take sights while frequently noting my DR positions.

"I caught a little flying fish in my cockpit today. If I had a dozen I would make a grand breakfast. Instead I put him on a hook and let my line out again to see if I could come up with something a little bit bigger. I wonder why no one has tried to surf to Hawaii. Well, as usual my final recording of the day is at the dinner hour.

"A nice orange sunset lingers in the distance, resembling a gigantic color wheel slowly changing from pink to orange, to butterscotch yellow, to red. Sunsets are my favorite time of the day. Wind is starting to pick up a bit. It was a quiet day today. I am encountering large, sporadic breakers, but so far so good. Lately I have been easing the long hours by reading a lot. Night comes and I pretty much slow down and try to sleep. Because I am trying to conserve on batteries I don't get to use my recorder to listen to tapes as much or read by flashlight. I used them a bit too much during the first week. You never realize how much something means to you until

CHAPTER FOURTEEN

you start running low.

"Utter calm is the word—tranquil. Even the seas have a good rhythm tonight. See you tomorrow."

CHAPTER FIFTEEN

Damage Control

Wednesday
July 7 – Day 27

LOG

0122
Course variable 240° – 255° magnetic
Rain off and on.
0300
Course variable 260° – 275°
Winds 30 knots. Turbulent motion.
0850
Clouds cover half the sky.
Newly refreshed winds 10 knots from the east.
Seas 4 feet.
1405
Winds have been light since 1100.
1830
Wind picking up out of the northeast,
anticipate a squall.
WE 28 seconds fast.
2000
Approximate position

CHAPTER FIFTEEN

23°20'N
142°02'W Rfx.
Cse – 265°
Rain and wind comes and goes. It now looks like there is an immense dark cloud approaching from the east.
2400
Heavy rains on and off.
Wind 30 knots from the east.
Swell 6 foot coming from the north.
78 nautical miles daily run
1450.4 total nautical miles traveled

TAPE

"Twenty-seven days out of Los Angeles. Over 1,300 miles traveled. I am near the 140 degree west longitude. Latitude, I cannot be too specific. I have been trying to complete a running fix, noon sights and arc of position sights, but they put me all over the chart. I know it is a pretty big area; wish I hadn't goofed up my sextant awhile back. I have been amazed at the number of sights that have been close to my DR. I have logged course and miles, traveled day and night. I have no qualms about my situation; everything is going really well.

"Today I had my first complete and utter shock; I actually broke one of my whisker poles. With a fair breeze from the east, I jumped up, shook the reef out of the twins, was hoisting sail when a whisker pole jammed in the padeye and

DAMAGE CONTROL

the clip end tore out of the aluminum pole. I sat for a second and stared at what just happened, I was about ready to throw myself overboard, when I dropped sails and immediately began to repair the damage. Using my hacksaw, I removed about three inches off the broken end, drilled new holes and pop riveted the end shackle back into place. After an hour I had the twins up with a reef. I intend to use only the reef from now on if the weather keeps up like this.

"I have logged over 220 miles in the past three days, averaging seventy-two miles a day with reefed twins. During the day I average between two to four knots, four knots in the gusts. Then during the night it really blows from 11:00 p.m. to 4:00 a.m. and I average four and a half knots. Like I've said before, I've been trying to do noon sights, but by the way the shadows fall on my boat I think I am already south of the sun's declination. The sun's declination is 22 degrees 30 minutes north. If I am already south of the sun's declination, then there's a good chance I'll miss the islands. Visibility isn't as clear as I thought it would be. The squalls come and blanket *Little Breeze* with rain for twenty minutes. Then the sky clears, the wind picks up and it's time to hang on and pray you don't get thrown broadside to some of the swells! With conflicting wind directions the boat gets thrown about quite a bit.

"Breaking the whisker pole showed me the importance of carrying proper tools: saws, sharp drill bits, etc. Proper tools will be my next big investment. It took me thirty minutes to drill through one-eight inch of aluminum. If I hadn't bought that ten dollar hand drill at the last minute, today's repairs might not have been completed—the same

CHAPTER FIFTEEN

with the hacksaw.

"I am having a problem with my companionway slide sticking. I have to beat on it sometimes and wouldn't you know it, the blasted thing came out of its track. I got it back in alright, but my next boat is going to have a good fitting, watertight hatch. I have been pretty lucky so far, but I would be soaked if the weather was rough all the time. Just the little bit of rain I get seeps through the bottom of my drop boards. I keep putting silicon and dolphinite into these little leaks but water still seems to find its way in.

"Unfortunately, in addition to all of those surprises, I'd had the unpleasant task of cleaning out a locker that stunk to high heaven! Some of my cheese stores had gone bad. With that done, I was gung-ho to put in some miles today.

"Well, it's nine o'clock and time for dinner. So without further ado this will be the end of July 7, 1982, aboard the *Little Breeze*, via transpacific, Los Angeles to Hawaii. This is your good friend, navigator, explorer Michael Mann signing off."

Thursday
July 8 – Day 28

LOG
0800
Averaging 260°
Winds brisk, overcast skies, seas rolling but calmer.
Fourth fuel canister gone.
1330
Wind and swell prevailing northeast.

Hazy featureless skies but warm.
1945
Cse – 265°
2400
Good winds but outrageous sets from the northeast pounding my starboard.
Shifting more weight to starboard side.
85 nautical miles daily run
1536 total nautical miles traveled

JOURNAL

Today has been a very slow day. I don't mean slow as in speed, because in fact I am making fantastic mileage, but I mean that the days slip into nights and nights into days.

As I draw near my destination, I feel repressed anxiety wondering if I am where I think I am on the face of this massive globe. My navigation has been by the seat of my pants and not precise. I have to keep telling myself that I am close or I might start thinking irrationally and make decisions that I may later regret, like when I went to raise my twins the other day. No, I am where I am and I'll get to where I am going in the time I've calculated under the present conditions.

I think I have mentioned that I am growing despondent over the food. I have begun to suffer from the lack of variety and wholesomeness. My bowels testify to this every day. I lack fiber and substance in what I eat.

I should savor every minute of every day because I can only live a moment once and then it is gone, the sun moving

CHAPTER FIFTEEN

across the sky, the occasional bird and glimpses of flying fish. The ocean as it has appeared in all its states will forever be imprinted on my mind. I have been pushing myself and *Little Breeze* to go faster and faster and now I am afraid I am beginning to lose the spirit of the trip that I had intended. It is much more work than I had anticipated!

I now dream of disembarking, of sights and sounds I will encounter, of what my next step in life will be. I am afraid I will look back and wonder why.

Tomorrow will be a day not unlike today and in fact I might as well copy these entries for the next three days. My current state of affairs could change only for the good—by sighting a ship, or for the worse—by something else breaking on board that would stop my forward progress.

TAPE

"It has been six days since I last sighted a sailboat. It is probably in Honolulu by now. I am still perplexed about my exact position. However, I am somewhat confident that I have approximately 750 miles to go. One way or another I will be a little north or a little south of the islands. I would like to come in from the north so that I can follow the trades in. I am still wondering where I am going to go when I get there. I don't know for sure. I never checked on dock facilities or anchorages. I plan on just blowing into the nearest harbormaster's office to see what he has to say. He might even give me a citation for unsafe passage, ha....!

"Listen to this for a minute (putting the microphone up to the mast step where some creaking and groaning noises have been coming from). That is my mast step making that noise. It has me a little concerned. I am going to remove the stereo from the interior cabin overhead and tighten down the bolts. It could just be the fiberglass giving a bit. The noise is coming from the area of the modification where we put in the two backup plates, sandwiching the fiberglass cabin top to reinforce this mast step area because the boat has no compression post.

"I am thankful Montgomery's fiberglass lay-up crew did a good job. *Little Breeze* is only the seventeenth boat built of the M-15 model.

"Nothing new to report. Have been trying to sleep. Many times I just doze intermittently. I already have seventy miles logged today at 9:00 p.m. The sun is starting to sink into the horizon. Directly overhead are pellucid skies. To the west a small squall is in progress. It is crystal clear to the east. I try to stay up as late as I can so that I will be able to sleep when I try.

"After all this time I still attempt to catch fish. I have been trawling a hundred-foot line behind the boat with twenty-feet of thirty-pound test monofilament leader, baited with some dead flying fish. I lost all my fishing lures the first week out and have just been using baited hooks. I have been watching the sea birds today and now I see why I am not catching any fish. The birds are diving into the water a hundred feet behind my boat and I bet that if I pull my line in now there isn't any bait left. The birds are probably following schools of fish. I just did not come prepared to do any real fishing.

"I wonder what is going on in the world today. It has

CHAPTER FIFTEEN

been twenty-eight days and I'm sure there has to be some international crisis somewhere. I wonder if we are at war in the Middle East. I wonder if Reagan has been shot again. What could be going on in California? The beaches must be packed. Stacy—Laurel—my little nephew Jeremiah—I hope they are having a good summer. It has been a long time. I figured I would be talking with someone by now. I haven't talked with anyone in twenty-eight days—absolute solitude—that is a long time! I thought I would be close to navigated waters by now. Another five days and I should be sighting ships and sailboats!

"I hope I am at the longitude 143 degrees west and I hope I am not any farther south than 23 degrees north. The way the sun has been rising and traveling across the sky overhead, I could be wrong. I may be a little farther south. Even though I have lost confidence in my sextant, I keep playing around with it to give me something to do. I am pretty confident of my longitude because of the sumlog I use to derive my DR position. No luck with noon or arc of position sights. If you don't have a good DR position to start taking the sight, then the sight is not going to work. I taught myself the noon sight on the trip. I had never had any sea experience taking sights, just three months of reading and a month of taking sights at the beach. It is quite an experience. My next boat will be at least thirty-six feet with all the luxuries—including passengers.

"I am content that I am more than halfway now. I could be doing better if I had brought gas for the motor during the calms I had at the start of the voyage. Gerry Spiess used his outboard engine to stay on schedule in his *Yankee Girl*.

"At least I haven't had to worry much about freighters. But I know that even after all I've been through, the last week is going to be the most tiresome and rigorous as I approach the islands. The wind and seas will start building as I get closer to land. I will find the twenty-foot seas everyone told me about. I have seen some really big swells, but none as tall as my mast which is twenty-four feet off the water. This is about all for now.

"This had been my best week. When I calculate it out on Saturday, I'll bet I have at least 500 miles logged. I have been doing real well on power. I will be switching over to my second battery soon; I figure I have about six or seven hours of power left on the present battery. If I were to keep my masthead light on for any length of time, like eight hours, the power would be gone. I've only enough power to use the red light on my interior compass when needed. So, in order to conserve on battery power I can't operate more than one instrument at a time. I hope the second battery is good after all this time. As for the portable tape deck, I only play about two hours per day. Saturday will be a party and I'll put on my tux and tails. Good God, I need a bath!"

Friday
July 9 – Day 29

LOG
0400
Cse – West
Good Breeze.
0600 – 0830

CHAPTER FIFTEEN

Cse – 280°
Can't sleep because mast step has been creaking all night. Cloudy skies.
Seas calm but the northwest swell is a killer.
1230
Wind from the east.
Shifted weight to starboard to compensate for a port list due to the north swell.
1445
Winds steady all day. Twins reefed.
Random clouds. Winds shifting to the northeast.
87 nautical miles daily run
1622 total nautical miles traveled

TAPE

"Here we are at our favorite time of the day, recording time. Another day same as the last day and the day before that. Have had the sails up nonstop for seven days now. My routine is slow and easy. I couldn't sleep last night; I was up every hour looking around and thinking about what I would do when I got to the islands. Many uncertainties about the future now.

"Lately my customary garb has been a t-shirt and cutoffs. No need for anything else even at night. *Little Breeze* seems to be riding much better now. Have been eating a lot lately, mainly from a lack of anything else to do. Had a cup of coffee and oatmeal this morning. For lunch, pork and beans, rice, mixed vegetables, and a can of tuna. Still looking forward to that thick steak when I get to Hawaii.

"I hope to get the use of some facilities to clean and reorganize before continuing my cruise around the islands. If any yacht club will give me access to their facilities, maybe I could talk to some of the members there about the islands and even do some sight-seeing, like sailing to Kauai and Maui. Then after a while I will see about shipping *Little Breeze* home and I may even sell her. Yes, I think it will be time for a much bigger boat—something I could live on.

"Have been pretty creative in combining an arc of position sight with a noon sight and a LOP from the morning which gives me a running fix approximately fifty-five miles southwest of my DR position. I have been plotting two track lines on my plotting sheets. One track line has been strictly a DR plot using only the average course and sumlog speeds throughout the day. With the second track line, I am using a mishmash of traditional navigation, sporadic LOPs, noon sights and arc of position sights to plot a fix. The differences between the two are not too far apart, considering that I lost confidence in my sextant after I fiddled with the adjustments on it a week ago.

"Just counting down the days now. Wish I'd see a little more traffic, even though I am happy my nights are carefree and I don't have to worry about collisions. I haven't seen a boat since last weekend. Who knows, maybe this Saturday I will spot something. Maybe they are passing me right now!

"Changed to my last 12-volt battery. I used up the power on the first battery last night. That was good; it lasted twenty-nine days. My back and joints are still sore. I could sure use a bath and some solid food. I look around my boat and see all the little things I hurried through and left looking

CHAPTER FIFTEEN

shabby. This is the first time I have ever done anything like this. I will remember and know better next time. I am really surprised how well everything is going. When I first hit the trades, I was paranoid about big waves knocking me over and torrential rains ripping the sails. Lately, I haven't thought twice about it. That is it for tonight, short session."

Following seas

(Opposite) Line drying, Laundry day, Cramped quarters

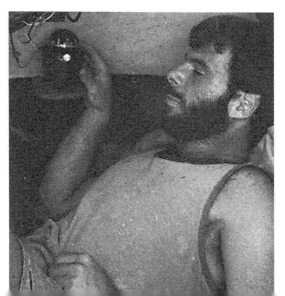

CHAPTER SIXTEEN

Running Under Bare Pole

Saturday
July 10 – Day 30

LOG

0430
Cse – W
Nice rolling swells from the east.
Steady breeze from the east. Clear skies.
Waxing crescent moon.
0930
Mackerel skies. Calm seas. Steady breeze.
WE 29 seconds fast.
1230
Wind steady 10 – 15 knots,
2 – 4 foot swell from the east,
6 foot swell from the northeast.
2030
Position Approximately
23°N
146°W

CHAPTER SIXTEEN

Winds steady.
Thin, wispy strands of cirrus clouds,
otherwise clear and warm.
81 nautical miles daily run
1703 total nautical miles traveled

JOURNAL

Yesterday was my friend Pete's birthday. How old is he now, twenty-five?

Today is my sister Stacy's twenty-first birthday. Boy how time flies. I would like to extend a hearty "Happy Birthday" to Stacy. Sorry I'm not there. I will send a card when I get to Hawaii. In fact, I will be writing a nice long letter to everyone as soon as I get on some nice steady terra firma, where things aren't shaking so much. There I will be able to write a decent, clean, handwritten letter. Stan, when I get back, we are going to party. We will sit back with these tapes and have a good laugh about this trip.

I am going to have to buckle down and start preparing myself a foundation to secure my happiness in the years to come. But what? What can I do? What can I accomplish? Where do my talents lie? I cannot be over the hill at twenty-two; I am still a young man. I should have prepared myself better. Now I am going to have to struggle and catch up.

When I graduated from Catalina Island School and entered Humboldt State, I was seventeen and ahead of the game. But I had no ambition and college was a struggle. I lost interest and only lasted a year. Then at Orange Coast College, my self-confidence returned. I felt good about myself and what I was doing. Marine Biological Consultants was an adventure and I enjoyed working there a lot. It was a challenge. But they had to let me go due to the lack of work. It wasn't their fault—the economy.

It didn't take long for me to bounce back and find another job that at least had regular hours and paid a decent, but only minimum wage. Again, this job had no future and so I soon found myself dreaming of moving on to new adventures.

I am sailing west at this time and I hope for the better. What will I do when I get ashore? Will it be the same or will I find some new opportunity? I have to do things for myself now. I have been lucky to have been able to pursue my interests so far.

Today is day thirty at sea. I find myself a real bore and lacking in intelligent conversation and ideas. I sit and complain about how screwed up my life is and how it has treated me unfairly.

"Happy birthday" Pete and Stacy!

TAPE

"Thirty days out of Huntington Harbor, actually twenty-eight days from Catalina Island. It is Saturday night. All is the same. Just had a well-earned bowel movement. It had been building up a few days. I was getting worried about the pressure and pain from constipation.

"I am sitting here going over my position and I am getting pretty desperate!

"Heading due west and I'm not able to do anything to get an accurate Rfx. I have just been trying to do noon sights

CHAPTER SIXTEEN

or high altitude sights. Both have been giving me somewhat vague positions. If I am being put south and west of my DR position that is all well and good, if that is where I am now. But to be safe and sure I will stick with my DR position which has been a little bit above the 23 degrees north latitude and currently west of 146 degrees longitude. My other sights have been putting me west of 147 degrees west and I am down around 22 degrees, 40 minutes north. Either way I know I haven't got but 600 miles until the islands, until I see something or someone! And then maybe a little bit more than that before I get to Hawaii.

"I am not too worried about my position; the sun has been rising right behind me and setting dead ahead lately. The sun's declination these days is twenty-two degrees, eleven minutes north and getting farther south every day, so I think I am close to that latitude. I might even be right where I should be when I approach the islands. I might be a little south and headed right for the Big Island or Maui.

"If I hit Honolulu first I will hopefully find a kindly yacht club that will be happy to see me and offer me their facilities for a few days. If not I will be beachcombing! I am a member of the Slocomb Society and my dad is a member of the Long Beach Yacht club and I would imagine that the Hawaiian yacht clubs would offer member reciprocity.

"Maybe I can talk to a few of the members and ask about the best place to shower and find a hose. I need to clean this boat up! I'm afraid of what I am going to find when I start pulling stuff out of the lockers.

"It is Saturday night and everything is still the same. I have been doing unbelievably good on miles. I haven't even touched the twins and haven't had to correct any kind of navigation. We are basically heading 255 degrees magnetic or with the variation added on 270 degrees west, true west. *Little Breeze* is sailing well, but getting knocked about a bit. Now and then she gets knocked a bit farther west, a little northwest. And sometimes she gets knocked a little south, a little southwest. But all in all I am pretty much heading due west. That is about where I stand position and navigation wise.

"I am getting real tired of my food choices. I'm at an emergency low on cigarettes; I won't have any choice but to quit soon. Otherwise, I will have to start smoking this parsley I have here.

"The reality of my present situation is no fresh fruit, no crisp vegetables, no tavern nights, no family and no friends. It is only me and the Pacific Ocean right now.

"God has it been something! Every day I get a little wiser and have become very deep in my thoughts. I have been reading my journal and have been besieged with more questions than answers. Where are you going? What are you going to do with yourself? What are you going to do when you get to Hawaii? I don't know!

"As I get closer to the islands I think about all the things I should have brought with me, but forgot. I should have taken more precautions. Things were really frantic prior to departure. I thought, oh God, if I don't go now I won't go at all. So I went. I did not bring enough batteries for my tape player. Stan, I can't thank you enough, this tape player has come in so handy. My in-dash recorder would not have held up. I just barely have enough 12-volt power to use my lights.

CHAPTER SIXTEEN

And I know if I had been using my tape deck it would have been gone two weeks ago.

"I will be starting my fifth week on the ocean alone—alone! Four weeks on the ocean! How many out there can claim as much? If it is a claim at all, I don't know!

"My next sailing trip will never compare with this. Five days, a week? No sweat. Let's go sailing. There have been a few times when I physically pounded the boat and yelled, 'I want to stop!' But I couldn't. I haven't had to really do anything, but sit here. The boat has done everything. If I were to fall off, the boat would show up on its own in Honolulu. Everyone would say, 'nice boat—where is the crew?' Oh well, another nameless victim of the deep.

"I haven't seen anything really. No sharks, no fish, no whales, nothing! I am tired of flying fish and birds. The days have been nice. Haven't had any rains for some time now, which is alright since things get a little damp when it rains. However, it is about time for my decks to get washed down, so anytime clouds. The weather has been beautiful. I took a nice long bath today. The water is warm. Can you believe I took two baths this week? I am beginning to feel civilized!

"Well, this is the end of the fourth week out alone and I should put some mileage on this tape. I brought 3 ninety-minute tapes on which to record this trip. In the beginning I was lax and shy about talking on the recorder. But now I am talking up a storm to make up for my lack of social interaction. I have almost used up about one-eighth of this side already. So I guess I'll call it quits for tonight, even though it is still early, only about 9:30 p.m. PDST or 6:30 p.m. for this longitude.

"I slept really good last night. I will sleep well one night; then I am up most of the next night. Read and read. Write and write. Just finished the book *Hawaii*, the historical account of the island's development. I am definitely going to look up the missionary and island history when I get there. The way Michener writes is interesting: drama, intrigue, and adventure. I both laughed and cried at times. All in all, a good book and the longest I have ever read. I can't wait to see the movie. I have got to stop talking or I will talk this whole tape out, bye."

Sunday
July 11 – Day 31

LOG

0830
Course still west.
1030
Position Approximately
23°N
147°W
Wind coming from the north. Seas calm to fair.
1434
Winds veer to the east.
Really tranquil this afternoon.
Should have raised twins, but getting dark soon.
1730
Winds picking up now. Skies flawless. Breeze good.
83 nautical miles daily run
1786 total nautical miles traveled

CHAPTER SIXTEEN

Monday
July 12 – Day 32

LOG

0500
At this point I am somewhere between 21 degrees and 23 degrees north latitude and 147 degrees and 149 degrees west longitude.
This is about as close as I can get, somewhere in this 120 square mile area, the size of Little Rock, Arkansas.
Strong breeze from the east.
Seas rolling.
Swells from the east.

1145
Full twins.

1246
Winds forcing me to steer southwest.
Clouds building.
Might be in for some showers later today.

1730
Winds still steady from the northeast.
Cloudy. Swell still calm.
Been sleeping.
Course has been swinging all over.
Put in reef.
Winds really screwy.

1930
Cse – 260° – 270° magnetic
Winds swung back to the east 15 – 20 knots.

Swell building north-northeast.
Even with full twins I couldn't do any better
than with the twins reefed.
2300
Have had no success with sights today.
Is discouraging but not hopeless.
I should be getting close,
should be hitting some traffic soon.
81 nautical miles daily run
1867 total nautical miles traveled

Tuesday
July 13 – Day 33

LOG
0200
Skies mostly clear. East winds 25 – 30 knots.
Seas getting tempestuous,
six foot swells from the east.
1000
Cse variable 270° – 240°
Skies clear. Swells 8 – 10 feet from the north
and northeast. Wind 20 knots plus, sun overhead.
1900
Cse – variable
Approximate position
21°48'N to 22°48'N
149°50'W to 150°40'W
No successful sights today. Winds good all day.
2358

CHAPTER SIXTEEN

Bare pole at 2 knots.
Heading 235 degrees to 245 degrees.
Winds gusting 35 knots from the northeast.
Sails down—Warp out! Rain.
Have been pushing the boat real hard.
Performance has been beyond reproach.
Even with variable wind and swell forcing helm hard over; self-steering will always compensate and bring the boat back on course, (except for a few freak north swells).
Now for some sleep.
94 nautical miles daily run
1961 total nautical miles traveled

TAPE

"It is really blowing at 2:13 a.m. It has been awhile since I had a blow like this. Things are rock-n-roll. I am surfing and skiing and sliding and twisting in every direction. I slept all day today, so that is why I am up so late. Can't really sleep anyway when it is this rough, because I am paranoid something is going to go wrong. Everything has been holding up except for my position.

"I did not get one good sight today, nothing even close to my DR position—that bothers me a bit.

"Saw what I thought could have been a jet passing from west to east off my starboard, some distance in the sky. I didn't think it was a star; it was moving too fast and blinking like the strobe of a plane. If it wasn't a plane, then I guess it was a UFO. If that is the case then this is my first UFO sighting.

"I broke into my survival pack and got my very last two cigarettes. I'm just sitting here contemplating what to do next. I have been reading my brains out; haven't wanted to do much else. I broke down and put up full twins for the first time in ten days. The winds were pretty light this afternoon. It didn't seem to make much difference. I still plowed along at four knots with the swell behind me, and then stalled down to about three knots on the backs. If I had my twins with a reef, I would have stalled at two knots. No big deal, I still only put in eighty miles. Yesterday, I put in eighty-one miles under the same conditions, except today the winds hung on from the north a little bit longer, which made self-steering difficult.

"An extraordinarily vast star field sweeps across black night skies; thousands and thousands of stars. Have been encountering a few squalls at night. They come, overtake you, and then blast you with rain for five to ten minutes. Surprisingly, it is clear skies again. If only the swell would stop coming from three different directions; I can handle a following one but when I get this north swell it knocks the daylights out of me!

"If I could just be confident of my exact position, I would feel much better even without cigarettes. Having smoked those last two, I've officially quit. I know I have to be close and getting closer. Almost 1,900 miles logged. It is reassuring, but anything could still happen. Actually, I am better off than I thought I would be. I thought I would be so tired, worn out and miserable that I could not even move. But I feel physically about the same as when I set out on this secluded adventure. I am not too happy about my eating, digestion and elimination lately. I still have strength in my legs and arms. A little sore, a little tight, with pains here and there, mainly from sleeping on these cushions. Other than that I feel pretty good. The wind is up and ripping. What I wouldn't do for a good eight hour sleep in a real bed that doesn't move! Don't even talk to me about water beds.

"It has been an unproductive day. Since I last spoke earlier this morning, I was able to sleep until 10:00 a.m. I woke up, logged my miles, tried taking a sight without success (not even close) and I began my daily reading. I read the book *Seagull* in a day and a half. Now I am reading *Thin Air*, another exciting adventure. I am glad I am not a speed reader or I would be in trouble.

"I have been having a peculiar pain today. A sharp pain central to my stomach that then moves to my chest and then back to my stomach and spreads out to the kidney area. It could be from food, constipation or lack of exercise. Exercise is hard to do on this rocking boat. If you don't have a hand on something or if you are not braced, then you're going to get thrown over against the side of the boat and it is going to hurt! To really exercise you have to have both hands free or lift yourself off the deck, and then you're really asking for trouble!

"High winds and high seas prevailed last night, but today is calmer. I have seen some immense swells, but I really can't tell their size sitting down in this little boat. Some tower over me and others come up from behind and roll under me. I'm really hoping to spot another plane and to be able to identify it better. I guess they're harder to see during the day.

"I have come to the desperate conclusion, due to the sun's travel across the sky and in relation to my position (declination from Almanac 21 degrees, 45 minutes north), that I have to figure my latitude this way. At noon shadows are straight down.

"I am afraid my approach to the islands might be a little awkward. If I am north of the islands heading south I can't miss, but if I am south of the islands heading west I could go fifty miles away from the islands and depending on the weather, I might not even see them. If I am north, I can probably run into some shipping traffic, but I am not sure of what would be coming south. My longitude, which I should be able to get from my morning and afternoon sight, hasn't even come close. I am more than a degree off, and as you can tell, this is not good. I am pretty sure my sextant has seen better days as far as alignment and calibration goes. I am just going to DR from here on out.

"I only have about another 300 or 400 miles to go. I have been doing eighty miles a day since Sunday. I have eighty miles logged now at 9:30 p.m. and a good 240 miles logged in the past three days. In just three more days I should be hitting something. I don't feel like eating or cooking now that it is so hot and humid during the day. Have just been eating cold fruit cocktails; I am losing my appetite altogether.

"The stormy weather has forced me to stay in the cabin on my back most of the time these days. I really should be sitting up, but I just can't handle the motion. If I sit in the cockpit, everything takes a beating; my teeth rattle and my guts get battered to death. Maybe I should have a motocross gut belt instead of just a seat belt. As far as the sunsets are concerned, since I am on Pacific Daylight Savings Time, they start around 10:30 p.m. I am confident about my longitude being 150 degrees west.

"In these trades I doubt I will see anything coming from the west, except for a plane or a freighter. Everything should be coming from the east. I'm getting a little paranoid, I should be in some traffic lanes but I still haven't seen any ship traffic. I am dying to talk with someone!"

Wednesday
July 14 – Day 34

LOG

0900
Cse – 230° magnetic
Warp pulled in around 0430. Wind still too much, swells calmer, skies clearing.
1045
Put up twins with reef.
1445
Course 240° – 250° magnetic
Winds steady 10 – 15 knots east by northeast,
15-foot swells from the northeast.
1830
Wind blowing northeast.
Always blows hard from the northeast.
Swells GIGANTIC!
2230
Same wind and a little stronger.
2341

Winds came up strong last night. Twins down.
No warp yet.
I came real close to blowing out sails today.
68 nautical miles daily run
2029 total nautical miles traveled

JOURNAL

And so I've let another few days go by as if I had never even lived them. Sorry to say no ships have been sighted, and speaking of sights, I have had little luck with navigational sights. How wonderful it would be to see an island by Friday—I have a chance you know. Less than three hundred miles and I should have a glimpse of at least the mountains or volcanoes on the Big Island. I have envisioned this sight over and over in my head for some time now. The only thing is I'm not sure in what direction I will see my dream come true. Will they be dead ahead? Or maybe off to port where they should be, but possibly off to starboard because I think I am that far south.

If I don't see the islands in at least 300 more miles, I will begin to have a terrible breakdown. I want to find those guys that told me "Yeah, no sweat, you can just drift to Hawaii after you get into the trades!" It is not that I am so worried about my position, but I would like to get some sign.

I am slowly becoming despicably low on goodies. No more granola bars. Almost out of bread and peanuts. All I have left in my food stores is chili beans, soups, stews, vegetables, and canned fruit. I am almost in a survival situation.

CHAPTER SIXTEEN

Well, it is 10:30 in the morning. The sun is out as usual. The day has begun. I grab my book and before you know it the day comes to an end.

CHAPTER SEVENTEEN

Unexpected Knockdown

Thursday
July 15 – Day 35

LOG
0329
Cse – variable 230° – 240 – 270° since 2400
It's been a nightmare!
Rain, gale winds and seas, WARP OUT!
0630
Course the same.
Conditions a little better.
0845
Cse – 210° – 310° no change
1645
Gale force winds with swells 8 – 20 feet,
east-northeast chop.
Was knocked down,
lost everything I had lying out in the cockpit!
22 nautical miles daily run
2051 total nautical miles traveled

CHAPTER SEVENTEEN

TAPE

"I hope I can talk at the end of the day. Three o'clock in the morning and I have just been hit by the most horrible storm yet, a full gale with at least forty-knot winds, heavy rain and heavy seas. It started off as the usual hard winds in the night and I just shirked it off. I didn't pay much attention to it. Outside I could see only dark ominous clouds in the distance. I pulled down the sails about midnight and started to drift as usual. This time I've been hit hard, really hard! I think I have been knocked down once—I hate to think about it.

"I am back upright, but on a list because my gear has shifted. Right now I am brewing a pot of coffee. I was comfortably sleeping. Then suddenly the seas were rolling big time and I could hear the wind howling through the rigging. A swell snuck up and knocked me over. Like I mentioned before, these north swells come up all of a sudden, rogue waves that knock you senseless! Well, I got hit by one of those waves and I know I was knocked down hard onto the port side. I was already riding a warp. Just in my underclothes, I immediately bailed outside, in the rain, to see if there was any damage. I changed the position of the warp and re-coiled my halyards and sheets that were trailing in the water. The mast and rigging were still intact. I got myself completely drenched; even got the cabin a bit wet.

"I am now inside changing into dry clothes and pumping out the five or six gallons of water that found its way into the bilges. Scared—let me tell you! I have no trouble admitting it. This is the big leagues. Not only am I worried about the weather, but I am also getting close to Hawaii and should be coming into some traffic soon. Ships are not going to see this pint-sized boat bobbing in the dark. The only thing going for me is that it is warm—the rain, the wind, everything is warm. God, let me make it until dawn!

"The nights have been hectic the past few days. The past two days have been terrible. I had a week of fair winds and calm seas going. Ever since the evening of July third, I never had to take down the sails. I may have had to head in a different direction than I wanted, but other than that everything was going great. Now the weather has been getting progressively worse. Last night when I took down sails, I knew I was in for something, but this was way more than I expected! Almost perfectly calm and all of a sudden the winds come on strong. You can hear it howling, it shakes the whole rig of the boat. What a grisly night!

"Right now I am in short pants and t-shirt, sitting next to my companionway. I have the strobe light tied off to the boom, blinking every two to three seconds. I am thinking very hard of a hundred million different places I would rather be, but I put myself here so I really can't complain. This is my trip, my breaking into manhood or my stupidity, one or the other. I don't know! I don't know what I would call it right now.

"I wonder how those large freighters ride these storms. Undoubtedly, size and mass are their friends. God, if we survive this I'm going to look into what it takes to train for a career on something much bigger than 15 feet.

"Just today I started reading a manual I have on survival navigation. I could consider myself in a survival situation, but as long as *Little Breeze* is sound and I have food, water,

CHAPTER SEVENTEEN

warm clothes, and a place to sleep I will be fine—this is fun!

"Masthead light is on, strobe is on, and the radar reflector is up. Warp is out. Thanks to the storm, I am heading due west—I'll be to Japan in another month. I almost have the supplies to do it too, but don't think I could last quite that long. I packed for sixty days and I am thirty-five days out. I should be able to last another thirty days.

"Only managed to put in sixty-eight miles yesterday. My mileage logged on the sumlog is 2,026 miles, as of midnight. None of this out here is what I expected. I guess I kind of underestimated everything. I was contemplating windy nights, big rolling swells, but not this chop from three different directions. Four-foot swells repeatedly from the east, then eight footers that bash the boat from the north and then occasional sets of two to three 20 footers from the southeast. Sometimes when the wind is blowing, the seas calm down, and when the wind dies, the seas are choppy. I'm going outside to take a look. *WOW baby*—the swells are *HUGE* but I'm not getting out a tape measure!

"It is somewhat comforting that the skies have cleared a bit over me. Despite what is going on in these seas, stars now cover the north area. I am really a dazed stargazer taking this all in.

"Man, oh man! It comes and goes. Can you hear it? Can you hear the pelting rain and the deafening noise of the sea out there? Can you hear me getting slammed by a swell? The force of the Pacific is exploding around *Little Breeze*. Some of these swells I am taking would knock anybody silly! When I am in the troughs, visibility goes from one mile to zero. I can't wait until daylight, being in the dark is a killer. There is no security at night when you can't see what to expect next. Being in such a mundane routine last week, I was a little slack about preventive maintenance. I almost blew out my sails tonight. Assuming that it was going to calm down in a minute, thinking it was only one of those gusts, I decided to raise the twins. But *NO!* It wasn't until the sails were being twisted around the forestay that I decided to pull them down. Right now they are wrapped in a saturated ball on deck forward, tied down with whatever loose lines I could find. I should bring them in, but I don't want all that wet sail in here. I don't even want to get out of this cabin and get up on the foredeck!

"There is nothing to munch on anymore. I ate all my snack items. Yep, things are in a sad state of affairs here. What do you do in the case of utter terror? If I could call somebody, I would, but I can't! There is nothing anyone can do for me right now. I just hope this big bathtub holds together. Just never know what to expect. I could easily sleep right now if everything would stay calm but the anticipation of what could happen next prohibits me from that luxury. I wish I could rest. Looks like I had better be on a pretty attentive watch now. With this amount of adrenaline going, I could probably do a few laps around the boat. I wish I had a smoke! I am sitting here praying, which I haven't done in a while. I don't know how, but God, please let me get through this night!

"Same day, same storm, same place I was five to six hours ago. Nothing has let up. I cannot put up sail. The seas are so high, I am really feeling fatigued. I forced myself to eat some oatmeal. A blinding sun is now coming through the portholes. The wind keeps coming incessantly—forty knots. My visibility is affected by the spray and the immense waves are as big as ever. I have no control over the situation, but I am able to stay dry and out of the weather. I hate being in this position. I am so close. I cannot see a thing on the horizon.

"I feel really funny. I must be barely sane to be able to sit here and tape all this. If I were having any psychological problems, I would be doing whatever senseless thing I would be doing. I can't seem to think on any one thing. I can't bring myself to do anything. I am sitting here like a vegetable. I don't know what I am supposed to do. Someone tell me! I can't sail. I can't row. The winds are intent on hurling us toward the islands. Walls of water are towering above the mast now. No matter what—I have to get some sleep.

"Started to doze, but that was a miscalculation! For the second time today, I was literally knocked awake to the most frightening scene imaginable! Breaking seas were relentlessly pounding the boat until suddenly, with one quick roll, I realized we had been knocked down to the point where I wasn't sure if *Little Breeze* was going to right herself. Time stood still. In unbelief I found myself standing on the port side of the cabin looking down at the ocean waters below boiling against the porthole. It was like looking through a glass bottom boat.

"There was no time to contemplate the situation. I braced my feet in the cabin footwell and lunged toward the starboard side using all of my weight to right *Little Breeze*. Loose gear that had shifted to the port side was thrown along with me. Thank God it is my habit to always keep the hatches closed or I would have been dealing with a much worse scenario.

"I want to get out of here—I really do—I really, really do! As much as I didn't want to venture outside again I needed to assess how *Little Breeze* was weathering the storm. As I peered out over the cockpit I realized I had made my first big mistake! I hadn't secured my loose gear in the cockpit and now my bucket, bailer, pot, cup and a cushion are gone, swept away into the deep! Thank God my bilge pump is working. My VDO seems to be intact, but it may have gotten some water inside the trip log gauge. Both compasses seem alright. Needless to say, the cabin is a little flooded. The motor is still on the transom; I feared it too had been ripped off by the waves.

"But I lost my stuff, my really important stuff! You just don't lose important survival equipment! That will teach me! I am less than three hundred miles from Hawaii and have become so cocky that I think all I have to do is sail this thing. Now here I am in the big ones! Right here, right now. This is it! I don't even know where I am. I knew this was going to happen; I knew that when I got close all hell would break loose. And sure enough, it has. I am so upset with myself for messing with the sextant. Upset at everything. Everything is saturated—I am awake now!

"It is now eight o'clock at night, same day, same conditions. It was calm for a minute. It is almost dark again. I wonder if the storm will last much longer. Either it is too windy to put up sail, or too much sea, or both. I feel funny. I feel lethargic and listless. I don't know what is going to happen to me. I need some nourishing food and some good

CHAPTER SEVENTEEN

sleep. I doubt I will get either one until I am ashore. No signs of anything.

"I am being pushed southwest, but I don't know at what rate. The warp is out so it is holding me back. With this storm, I could be anywhere!"

Friday
July 16 – Day 36

LOG
0100
Heading 230°
Back to the usual pattern (it seems) riding warp again tonight.
0800
255°
Pulled in warp. Seas smooth.
Wind about 25 – 30 knots.
0900 – 1030
Winds picking up, really pushing us along.
1040 – 1304
Heading averaging 230°
Pulled in warp around 0200.
Put up twins.
1806
Winds and seas building (took down sails).
Bare Pole!
2030 – 2200
Heading 270° – 280°
Sailing myself for awhile.

Bare pole, keeping west.
2400
Still bare pole but not for long
51 nautical miles daily run
2102 total nautical miles traveled

TAPE

"I haven't been doing very well the past couple of days. I made twenty-two miles drifting yesterday. Not so much that I can't sail, but these past five days I was only able to make 400 miles. I could have done 500 – 600 miles. I will log up the miles tomorrow. I am bare pole doing two knots, which is really more than two knots. For the past week I've been plotting my DR and circling my position with a sixty mile radius, so I am somewhere in there. If I am at the upper limit, I will have no problem hitting Kauai. If I am at the lower limit of my DR position, I should have no problem hitting the other islands.

"My DR position is 22 degrees north, 153 degrees west, coming up on 2,100 miles traveled. If I sail just one or two more good days, I will know if I am close. The islands should be right over the horizon. Bare poling, I've just tied off the tiller center and am letting the wind drive me in. Well they did tell me that you could drift to Hawaii once in the trades. That is exactly what I have been doing the past two days.

"Everything is coming out of the east going west right now. As long as that continues, I don't fear being knocked sideways and broadside again.

"I put up the sails about four hours today, but it was too

gusty. Self-steering. Swells are down from yesterday's which were at least twenty feet. You couldn't even take a picture to capture the size of those swells. The rain and squalls have been hectic, but it's the swells that really scare me! Right now the winds are really screaming. My eyes are burned out from reading during the day. I haven't had much sleep the past few days, catching an hour here, an hour there. I stand atop my cabin now searching the horizon, looking for smoke from a freighter, sun reflecting off a boat or plane, or the speck of a mountain over the clouds.

"Lately I have been roughly estimating my location. No sights. I'm sure I'm somewhere in my circle approximation. I'll know in a couple of days. Hopefully by Sunday I will have a better picture of the situation. I should have made contact and if not, well, I'll have to start plan B, *survive*! I will hook up my AM-FM stereo to see if I can pick up any local radio stations. I should also be able to pick up the VHF weather station when I'm close. I am still hanging in there, nothing much more I can do. In dire need of some fast-food staples—hamburger, french fries, milkshake, ice cream, and ice cold milk. One good development, I did catch sight of a very large flock of birds. I saw three or four dozen attacking some kind of schooling fish around me. I've seen some plastic trash floating by—all good signs to keep me going. I guess I am getting close."

CHAPTER EIGHTEEN

"We Read You Broken and Weak"

Saturday
July 17 – Day 37

LOG
0900
Heavy rains. Warp out.
Winds just a bit too gusty,
4-foot swells from the east.
0900 – 1445
Position Approximately
21° – 22°N
154° – 155°W
Warp in. Twins up in the reef.
ETA 48 hours!
2214
Approximate position
21°55'N
154°14'W
Wind east 10 – 12 knots. Swells 6 – 8 feet.
2400
Wind and swell still the same.
62 nautical miles daily run
2164 total nautical miles traveled

CHAPTER EIGHTEEN

JOURNAL

Time is 2:28 p.m. I just made verbal contact with Coast Guard channel on 16 and 22. They could hear me weak and broken. They said I was a hundred miles plus from the Big Island. (I knew that.) I gave them my approximate location, destination, description and told them that I had no emergency. This is how that conversation went:

VHF Channel 16: "Any vessel! Any vessel! This is the sailing vessel *Little Breeze*, Whiskey-Romeo-Tango-4-5-1-6—come in—over!" My heart missed a beat. I felt numb all over in anticipation. A second seemed like a lifetime."

"This is Honolulu Com Stat to the sailing vessel *Little Breeze*. Can we be of assistance?"

"You bet! This is the *Little Breeze* from Los Angeles, unsure of my position, and you are the first person I have talked to in thirty-seven days!"

"*Little Breeze* we read you broken and weak, can you try channel 22, channel two-two—over?"

"Roger, switching channel two-two."

I switched to channel twenty-two and I could hear the Coast Guard calling, but they did not receive my replies. I wasn't surprised.

"*Little Breeze* can you increase your power?"

"Negative, handheld VHF."

"*Little Breeze* do you have alternate communications, CB?"

"Negative."

"Short Wave?"

"Negative."

"EPIRB?"

"Negative."

"*Little Breeze* stand by."

So I waited. Picture me eagerly climbing my mast with my 9-volt, 3-watt, handheld transmitter trying to increase my range and reception.

"*Little Breeze* answer the following questions three times until acknowledged. Question one. Give us your personal description."

"My name is Michael Mann, age—twenty-two, five feet nine inches, 150 pounds, black hair, hazel eyes and a beard."

"Question two. Describe your vessel."

"Fifteen feet. I repeat a fifteen-foot, ivory, fractional, fiberglass sloop with lapstrack hull. Presently flying blue and yellow paneled twin jibs."

"Repeat your overall length?"

"Fifteen feet!"

"Are you from Honolulu?"

"Negative. Los Angeles to Hawaii. Thirty-seven days in transit."

"Question four. What is your position?"

"My approximate position is two-one degrees north, one-five-four degrees west."

"Roger *Little Breeze*. We read you broken and weak. It appears that you are on the perimeter of our transmission range one hundred miles from the Island of Hawaii."

I knew that!

"Last question. Are you in an emergency situation? Do you require assistance?"

"Negative, Honolulu. I repeat I am not in distress, just

CHAPTER EIGHTEEN

unsure of my position."

"*Little Breeze* stand by."

As I stood by my last set of batteries for the radio expired! I was left alone again—but at least someone knew I was out here, and I knew that my voyage was near its completion. For the next twenty-four hours and eighty miles, I maintained a watch in search of signs indicating any of the islands.

TAPE

"I just made contact with Honolulu rescue in Hawaii. It was by accident. I was scanning VHF radio frequencies when I picked up the weather station from Honolulu. It sounded real close, real clear. It says on the charts that they only have a forty mile range. I made a call on channel 16, just to see if someone would respond, so I could have a voice communication to check my radio. To my surprise, the Coast Guard jumped in on the line. They wanted to find out more about me, but they couldn't pick me up very well. I think they are a little concerned right now, one reason being that I do not have an EPIRB (Emergency Position Indicating Radio Beacon), the distress radio tracking transmitter that aids in the detection and location of boats. I gave them the description of the boat and myself, as well as our approximate position, but they could only tell me I was approximately one hundred miles off the Big Island. Maybe they'll send a plane over to see if I am where I said I was. Right now everything looks real good. They think I won't have any problems sailing into the islands.

"I hope I don't get that storm reportedly coming in

from the south. Before the Coast Guard came onto the VHF radio, I did pick up the Honolulu weather station operated by NOAA Weather Radio, a service of the National Oceanic and Atmospheric Administration. This broadcast originated from the Honolulu weather station. A great feature of NOAA is their ability to receive up-to-the-second severe weather information. They reported thirty-knot winds and twenty-foot seas in the Hawaiian channels. I don't doubt it. I made contact. I'm close!

"I caught three dozen flying fish in the cockpit this morning, probably because of the wind and rain from the storm last night. So I melted a big glob of margarine and deep fired those little guys whole. That was the tastiest meal I've had in a long time! I could have been here even faster if it had not been for that week of calms and three to four days' worth of storms. I have no idea what the weather will be like tonight or tomorrow. At least I won't have to worry the folks back home much longer.

"Oh the dreams I've had. If I am that close, I probably will have to stay up the rest of the time to keep an eye out. I can't believe I haven't seen any ships or fishing boats, or planes or anything.

"Feeling really good. I'd feel even better if the Coast Guard would send a boat or plane out to spot me.

"Told them I was in no distress; there was no problem here. The VHF I bought didn't last like the guy said it would. It is a good radio, but the power doesn't last. I used it about two hours, and then lost power. I'll wait until I see the island before using it again. I cannot leave it on to listen. The Coast Guard is probably still trying to contact me. Little do they know I'm not able to leave it on. I told them I was only fifteen feet. What did they expect that I would have a ham radio set?

"Anytime, anytime now!

"I knew that these last hundred miles would be the most difficult. Storm after storm! Here comes the rain. As long as the wind doesn't pick up, I'll be all right. I wonder; did I just imagine that whole conversation? It had been so long since I talked with anyone. It did feel normal. Starting to smell a little stuffy in the cabin these days. I hadn't noticed, or I haven't wanted to notice. But after taking that wave in here, things have started to smell pungent. No one could spot me in this squall right now!

"Ten o'clock at night and the sun is still out. No visual contact. Unsuccessful noon sight. Cloudy. Approximate position 22 degrees north, 153 degrees, 45 minutes west. I hope I don't pass the islands, I shouldn't. I should spot them tomorrow if I keep this up.

"Winds fifteen knots, swell four feet out of the east. Good weather today, except for the short squalls, short five minute blasts of wind that come up and are quickly gone.

"Feeling pretty good about everything and looking forward to seeing land. Actually I am in no hurry—I would like to have calm seas from here on out. The Hawaiian channels look like they may be the hardest part of the trip, because now there will be land to run into it. Reading the charts, I see Kaiwi channel can be as shallow as twenty- to thirty-fathoms. I can't make an error in navigation, so that means no more 300-foot warps out in any big winds because the warp could foul on the bottom in shallow waters.

"Actually, in some cases I am able to do pretty good just

bare poling. In this wind and weather last night I was getting pushed 2 – 3 knots; I had to steer myself for a while, but shoot, that's sailing isn't it?

"I am on my third and last tape. Plenty of food and water are left over. I could even stretch it for another twenty days, but I don't feel like trying that. I can't believe I was so calm when talking to the Coast Guard. It had been thirty-seven days since I actually talked to a human being. I was blown away inside—I really was! Next big step is to see someone waving at me and my *Little Breeze*.

"Well I am nearing the end. I would like to give my thanks to friend Marc Hightower, for all he has done for me. With his advice and direction I was able to put together a seaworthy craft. His help led to my proper planning of food stores, navigation, sailing technique and rigging. To Jerry Montgomery, I am grateful for his encouragement and enthusiastic expectation of the trip, the use of his shop facilities for final preparations, plus donated materials. Hope he had a good trip to Mexico while I was out here. I'll be giving him a call when I get in. My thanks to Stan Susman for the tape deck I've taped on and listened to all my music on and much more. Thanks to his advice and encouragement, and all his gang at Captain's Locker, Newport Beach, California. I give all a hardy thank you. Well, looks like I made it—Yaaaahooooo! To my other friends that doubted me, but had faith in my plans, thank you. And I am eternally grateful to my parents for their patience, understanding and help in my preparations. It was a group effort. I really couldn't have done it all alone. I think I have a better understanding of what it takes to plan for a long distance voyage. Your life is

CHAPTER EIGHTEEN

sort of a voyage and you're continually making preparations for that. I am looking forward to getting back to the mainland to see what opportunities I may now have.

"I will hit the first island I can and from there I'll head for Lahaina. The Hawaiian names are going to be a killer. I thought I would have much more to say when I got here. I was going to see the island come into view and I was going to describe all this neat stuff, describe my adventures and what they meant to me. I think it has just been one of those things. Another escapade, a day in life you only live once. Interesting, like I said, and I will be able to relate back after listening to these tapes. I feared for my life several times during this voyage. I questioned every minute of the trip. Yes, sensory deprivation (ha, ha, ha). Okay, that's enough. This is July 17, thirty-seven days out from California, over 2,100 miles out and less than 150 miles from visual contact of the islands—probably less than one hundred miles. This is Michael Mann reporting to you from inside the cabin of the *Little Breeze*. It is still light out at 10:09 p.m. (PDST)."

CHAPTER NINETEEN

WHAT ISLAND IS THAT?

Sunday
July 18 – Day 38

TAPE

"Today is Sunday, July 18, 1982. This is the *Little Breeze*. Last night was a good night. Steady breeze and smooth swell from the east. I stayed up most of the night to be sure I didn't run aground. I have made sightings. I spotted a jet last night. There was a nice large glow in the distance off the port to the south. Most likely a city with red flashing beacon lights in the center, but too far away to identify. Right before sun up, I spotted lights from what I guess to be fishing boats spread out along the coast. I'm still heading southwest, approximately 255 degrees true. The sky is a clear expanse directly above me, but the surrounding horizon is laced with hazy clouds. Expecting rain today. Sunrise will be in another half hour. The lights are beginning to dim and vanish into the horizon.

"I am thinking about changing to the fore and aft rig after breakfast to see if I can do a little broad reaching toward the south. Hopefully by this evening, I will be in port. If not, then I will heave to overnight.

CHAPTER NINETEEN

"I can't tell you what an exhilarating experience this has been! It is still not over; I'll bet the hardest part is still to come. I am looking forward to fulfilling my cravings for hamburgers, ice cream, sodas, an icy cold glass of milk, and any additional goodies I can get my hands on. Maybe I'll just sit back and listen to these tapes for a couple of hours. I hope my engine will run after thirty days. I am already making a list of things I need to do when I get there. I will have to clean up and get reorganized which will probably take as long as it did to get ready. Have several things to do: motor maintenance, boat maintenance, personal maintenance, and correspondence. All need immediate attention. I still don't know where I am. It doesn't matter now. I don't care. I didn't miss, that's for sure! Yes indeed—I didn't miss!

"Unless they have oil rigs out in the middle of the Pacific that no one knows about, I am sure I am off the islands. A little bit north and a little farther west than I anticipated. I don't know if that is the Big Island off my port. I would like to head for Maui first. So I am going to keep on this tack until the sun comes up and I get a clear picture of the situation. It would be grand if I could get twenty-five- to thirty-miles visibility today, but I highly doubt it. I am going to start heading south; I am approximately 21 degrees north, 155 degrees west. I see nothing off my starboard or to the north. Clear skies in that direction, although there are clouds hugging the islands. Mauna Loa volcano is 13,000 feet; I should be able to spot that but not right now. The highest point on Maui is 10,000 feet, so I will need to get closer to see that. This could be it; I'm going to start getting things squared away and head south.

WHAT ISLAND IS THAT?

"After breakfast, the sun came up and in the distance I spotted land at last—I was overjoyed! Dropped my twins, put up my main, with both reefs in, and the storm jib, because it was already blowing twenty-five knots, and steered a 170 – 190 degree magnetic course.

"My first sight was the silhouette of a gradual sloping landmass in the distance. It was, of course, one of the Hawaiian Islands, but I didn't know exactly which one it was. I thought to myself, maybe this could be Maui.

"I beam reached against the easterly wind that had for so long been my pride and joy, for so long, my friend. Now the wind and swell had become my enemies—I had to fight them. It was impossible to let *Little Breeze* self-steer and I was forced to steer by hand. I was soaked to a point I hadn't experienced this whole voyage. As I began my turn toward the island, my knot log read 2,232 miles. After another ten miles I got closer and could see a white structure on one hillside and the entire shape of the island. The land was high at both the west and east ends with a gradual sloped valley in between. I was thrilled that I was finally making headway! I told myself I would be in port tonight.

"I persisted to make for land. After a while longer I ran across a trolling boat. My first boat! I could see real, live people on the boat. I waved and waved and waved, but no response. So what! I kept cruising. To the southwest I noticed a gorge in the coastline that might just be a spot for a marina. I knew I was on a north shore, but which island?

"As I approached the island, still heading south, I passed more fishing boats. This weather couldn't be described as fishing weather. Using my binoculars to obtain a closer

CHAPTER NINETEEN

view, I could see that the shore in the distance was as I had thought—barren beach. Now discouraged that I couldn't spot a marina, I headed for what looked like a cove, a good snug pocket where I could kick back and rest. As I headed that way I noticed a boat nearby trolling slowly into the swell. I am going to ask them, I thought. I turned *Little Breeze* around and would have sailed right into them, if they hadn't replied! I dropped my storm jib and under twin reefed main, I heaved to. Waving emphatically, I yelled, 'I need directions. I need help!' That was the first time I had said 'help' other than yesterday when I asked the Coast Guard for the same kind of directions.

"The fishing boat did a complete circle and came around toward me. I yelled over to them, 'I'm Mike Mann. I'm thirty-eight days out of Los Angeles. I am not sure where I am. Can you tell me what island that is?' To my total surprise and utter amazement, can you believe they said it was *Oahu!* That island that I thought was Maui, on the longitude I was so sure of, actually is west of my estimated longitude. As far as latitude, I still knew I was between 21 degrees to 22 degrees north.

"Not only did I pass Maui, the Big Island, and Molokai, but I could have passed Oahu! It appears I made a very good decision by turning south at the first sight of land, which I had thought was a mere speck.

"As I approached the island, I saw nothing but beach. I headed in that direction, thinking it would be the best place for harborage. It turned out that the point of land I was heading for was Haleiwa, the most serene, the most picturesque and most Hawaiian of ports I could have entered to begin my stay in Hawaii. It was breathtaking as I sighted the first flash of green over the unpopulated north shore area—beautiful! It wasn't just the north shore and rolling green grasses over the red volcanic earth, but it all appeared magical as I began my approach on a reach.

"Between the winds and the swells, I had an awful difficult time steering when my self-steering failed me. After thirty-eight days solo at sea, you would think I would have no problem sailing. I had my hands full and I was soaking wet. It was so warm that none of that mattered.

"I sailed into the harbor looking for an official dock, but didn't see any so I anchored behind the breakwater. It has a medium shell bottom and adequate for using a 4-pound Bruce anchor with 35-feet of quarter-inch chain and 100-feet of 5/16-inch yacht braid.

"The fishing boat that I had asked directions from came by. I waved. They told a few of their friends about that little sailboat asking directions. Several of them were interested and started asking questions about me, my boat and my adventure. Believe me, I will tell them some tales. I feel really good about the whole trip!

"We made it! *Little Breeze* and I made it!

"Arrived, anchored Haleiwa!!! 1800 Hawaii-Aleutian Daylight Time (HADT)."

Monday
July 19

TAPE

"I was very naïve thinking that all the planning and

preparation and diligent navigation would actually bring me to Hawaii.

"I almost missed this island! If I had missed this island I would have missed it all. Was that fate, luck or destiny? Right now I am sitting in my boat in Haleiwa, a snug comfortable little community for both the locals of Hawaii and those who came from the mainland. They seem both friendly, yet reserved. I have been able to find a dock where I can unload and get my act together.

"And so ends my 38-day trek across the Pacific. Hurray! My sumlog total reads: 2,260 nautical miles. Just a coincidence since I had miles already on the sumlog before departing California.

"Haleiwa is not a commercial harbor but a small sport fishing and public boating marina. There is a park to the southwest, grassy and green. Sea and surf. Nice. To the south, inside the breakwater, are several rows of docks. A finger of land with a harbor office on the end cuts right into the otherwise negotiable harbor. There is a navigation light in the distance flashing every ten seconds: Kaena Point to the west, Kahuku Point to the northeast, and Kam highway is the main drag.

"I am here. I am happy. And I am going to try to get a good night's sleep. Tomorrow I will try to do as much work on *Little Breeze* as I can while I have the slip.

"I made it, perhaps with the help of providence. I made it because of my desire and dreams of accomplishment. I don't know exactly my frame of mind, but I know I was in good conscience.

"Now what? Where do I go from here?"

Wednesday
July 21

JOURNAL

Looking back on my arrival I will say that the last four days were the toughest, but it was definitely all worthwhile when I touched land on Sunday for the first time in over five weeks. I felt the excitement, that rush of emotion and accomplishment I had so long been looking forward to. How beautiful the island is—Oahu!

There were no crowds to greet me as I came into this little marina of Haleiwa, containing no more than fifty boats. I sailed by the little Japanese ladies fishing off the end of the docks and I definitely felt as if I were in a foreign land. I tried to ask them where a guest dock or Harbor Patrol office was, but they spoke something in broken English that I couldn't understand. So I sailed over and anchored by another boat near the entrance, but inside the marina.

It was there while gathering my thoughts I was interrupted by, "Ahoy there *Little Breeze*. Are you the boat in from Los Angeles?" I turned around with my hands in the air in triumph. He asked, "Did you really sail that little boat here from L.A.?" I proudly replied, "Sure did!" His response was, "You da-man! Come over here. I want to buy you a beer!"

I grabbed my flip flops and dove in. It was the first time I had been swimming in over a month, but the fifty-foot swim from *Little Breeze* to the breakwater felt amazingly good! As I climbed up onto dry land for the first time since I pushed off the dock in Huntington Harbor, I felt a little wobbly in

CHAPTER NINETEEN

the knees, but after a few strides and the thought of being able to talk with someone face to face, I quickened my step. This man was fresh from Orange County himself, he began introducing me around and now I know quite a few people. Mike, a local sailor, is another who has taken me under his wing. He managed to get a dock for me to tie up to so I could clean up *Little Breeze*.

Later that night, he took me to the Ice House where the native local fishermen hang out and we had some fresh fish. I haven't been able to remember the names of the local fish yet, but basically they are tuna and mahi-mahi. After that he took me to the Sea View Restaurant for salad, milk and MaiTais.

It has been thirty-eight days since I've eaten a decent meal and my desperate need for real food had to be fulfilled before I attempted to make contact with my family. I had been working on writing letters all the way across the Pacific but I knew they would want to hear my voice and be assured that I had finally made it to Hawaii safe and sound.

At 11:00 p.m., California time, I placed a call to my dad. He was so relieved and wanted to hear everything about my voyage. Boy, did I have a lot to tell him! I know that my enthusiasm helped relieve some of the stress he had felt as the family waited for news of my whereabouts.

Dad's group of friends at the Long Beach Yacht Club had tried to persuade him to disown me—I guess they figured it would help. You know the old adage, out of sight, out of mind, the idea that something is easily forgotten if it is not in our direct view or if we don't talk about it. Dad said they had not asked even once if he'd heard from me the entire voyage.

Many of those friends at the Yacht Club were seasoned sailors. They had told my dad, "No way will he be able to sail from Huntington Beach to Hawaii! He doesn't have the experience needed!" My dad had hope in the preparations I had made, but figured after all this time I might be getting urgently low on supplies.

The entire family had been anticipating that I might make contact with passing ships. When not hearing from me they were getting pretty worried.

I had no luck reaching my mom. Dad said she was away at a bridge tournament. Mom must have been able to get over her anxiety to some extent if she was able to go and concentrate on a bridge game. News travels fast, so I expect everyone will soon know that *Little Breeze* is peacefully anchored in Hawaii!

Marc was my next call. My first words were, "Success, everything went according to plan. All you told me about the winds, currents and sailing were accurate enough so that when a new situation arose, it was like I had done it all before, but I hadn't really. It was just a reflex reaction."

He told me the waiting had gotten to be too much for him and he called my mom on day thirty to see if she had gotten any word from me. She panicked and assumed that I was overdue. He quickly managed to reassure her that he was only calling in case I had arrived early. Inside he was worried sick that something may have gone wrong.

Marc got a kick out of reminding me how I came by my *Little Breeze*. Marc was to receive a Montgomery 15 as payment for work he did tooling up the new model boat.

CHAPTER NINETEEN

He wanted to buy the "World Cruiser Montgomery 17" but Jerry Montgomery didn't want to pay him cash or apply the 15's value towards the 17. Jerry noticed my interest in the Montgomery 15 and suggested that Marc "unload" the boat on me and use the cash from the sale towards the world cruiser M-17 he had his heart set on. Turned out to be the best unloading he could have done for Jerry.

That night I slept safe and sound. I felt as if I had found home.

Finally safe to jump in

(Opposite) Welcome to Hawaii, At the Dock, Time to regroup

We made it! Little Breeze and I made it!

CHAPTER TWENTY

WHAT HAPPENS NEXT?

Saturday
July 24

JOURNAL

Today I am anchored in the surfer's legendary Waimea Bay, although the surf is currently nonexistent.

On Monday I had begun the back breaking job of unloading, cleaning, and repacking. I was almost about set to begin my cruising, but I needed to get my motor running and find a new pot to cook in that would fit my little stove.

For the past three days, I have had dozens of conversations with the locals. They all call me crazy but it doesn't bother me anymore.

Wednesday, while working on the boat, both the News 9 team and a Channel 13 crew came by with their cameras and interviewed me. I was able to catch the news at 7:00 p.m. that night. I looked pretty funny but my *Little Breeze* looked good!

Thursday, no luck with my motor, but yet another news team stopped by to see what made this impulsive young guy sail 2,260 miles solo in a fifteen-foot boat. Unfortunately, I missed seeing myself on television that evening.

I finally was able to talk with my mom and of course she cried. I think the tears were a combination of both joy and relief.

That is all for now, just wanted to get something down. I will be writing letters back home and a little recap of my trip for Jerry.

Monday
August 2

JOURNAL

I have had a quiet and peaceful stay here in Kaneohe Bay. Although I am basically alone, I have met a lot of new people and their conversations and friendships make all that I do worthwhile. Of course many people question why I made the trip. Others want to know how I could stand being totally alone for thirty-eight days and wonder if I ever doubted that I would make it.

No, I never had any doubts about making it. After reading Gerry Speiss, *Yankee Girl*, I saw that other sailors could do it. I never thought of it as not making it, rather I thought only of the best way to make it in my fifteen-foot *Little Breeze*. I did have concerns regarding the duration of the voyage and possibly getting sick or injured en route.

Marc Hightower and Jerry Montgomery were really the only people who encouraged me. Their support was invaluable. The why of my trip isn't just because I knew I could do it or for the great adventure of it. Rather I needed to prove myself worthy of respect and mature enough to accomplish what few have, both to my family and for my own personal journey.

Letters from home arrived, brimming with news and encouragement. The letters from my dad were filled with words I have so needed to hear; he begins his writings with "To my sailing son—Michael."

It was difficult for my parents to let me set out on my own that June 11th. They opposed the voyage from the first day I told them of my intentions. Maybe after all the teenage years of rebellion they now realized I needed to find my purpose in this life. Regarding Dad, he must have realized that I was leaving Huntington Harbor happier than I had been in years.

The words of his first letter to arrive here in Hawaii still echo in my mind, "I'm very proud of what you have done and what you are doing. It is a real accomplishment although, as you have said, you did it for yourself. Still, it might be the type of thing that can open some doors for you—so don't hesitate to use it—you have earned it."

Within two weeks of my sailing into Haleiwa marina, my dad sent a letter to the Independent-Press Telegram, the local newspaper in Long Beach, telling them of my voyage. He even included some of the photographs I had mailed to him. The boating editor expressed interest in talking with me upon my return to Long Beach.

CHAPTER TWENTY

Monday
August 9

JOURNAL

I decided to head over to Lanai. Unfortunately, I almost started out too late for a peaceful passage. I was beam reaching parallel to the swells and although it was a little wet, I had only my main up with both reefs. Once behind Lanai, I thought I would be becalmed, but no! I was able to get a break from the four-foot seas; however the winds were at thirty knots and my mast head was now wiping back and forth like a bamboo pole. I thought for sure this would be the breaking point. Just two miles out of Kaunakakai, Molokai I was pretty tempted to turn back but I'm so glad I didn't.

Amazingly, it has been a great time in Kaunakakai. I was warmly greeted by the pineapple barge crew who over the course of a couple days gave me a dozen pineapples. They were quite excited to hear about my trip. In fact, all the Hawaiians I have met have been enthusiastic about it. They tell me how much they respect me, they give me praise but I don't need praise for something I like to do.

Haven't written in my journal for a while. The reason I guess is that I have used the time to clean up the boat and myself. My days now are filled with working on the *Little Breeze*; I got a charge on the battery, tuned the rig and found much needed gasoline.

Wednesday
August 11

JOURNAL

With the close proximity of Molokai and Lanai, I am able to sail easily between the islands. I had one of my better passages Monday. Although I only motored, it was short and sweet. While tying up at the dock, I met an interesting sailing couple, Dean and Suzie, and their friend Bruce. They were fellow sailors who were interested in my trip. They took photographs of me and *Little Breeze.* Perhaps something will come of this since Dean writes articles for the sailing and marine magazine, Lat 38.

I have been docked in Black Manele Bay, Lanai the past three days. Manele itself is divided into two areas known to the locals as White Manele and Black Manele. White Manele, with its beautiful white sandy beaches and enticing blue water, is a Marine Life Conservation District, but all a visitor needs to know is "look but don't take" and "pass through but don't anchor." White Manele is a haven for millions of tropical fish, and the snorkeling, I hear, is fantastic. Reefs large and small separate into underwater caverns filled with sea life.

Yesterday I ventured to Lanai City which is centrally nestled high on top of the island. There was a cool trade breeze blowing through the fir trees that surrounded the town. The aroma of pine and the cool, fresh air was almost intoxicating. It was here that I saw the Dole pineapple fields. As far as the eye could see, row upon row of island wide plantation pineapple. Lanai is known as the pineapple capital of the world.

Lanai is so much like Catalina Island (where I spent my high school years). Dry, low shrubs, sage and chaparral type vegetation abound. Yes, I definitely could enjoy sailing the rest of my life.

Wednesday December 15

JOURNAL

My days are more active and life has taken over. I've exhausted my search for adventure. The thirty-eight days sailing over were chock-full of adventures. I found out on arrival *Little Breeze* and I were followed by Hurricane Daniel across the Pacific.

The word "adventure" has several meanings. One meaning is encountering danger. Another is to take a risk or a challenge. *Little Breeze* and I had no choice in the adventure of Hurricane Daniel. We sure had a heck of a ride starting around the thirteenth of July and easing up around the seventeenth.

According to the National Weather Service, Hurricane Daniel formed as a tropical depression south of Mexico with winds of twenty-five to thirty knots on July 7, 1982. Moving west-northwest, Daniel slowly intensified into a tropical storm around noon on July 8, with winds of thirty–five to sixty knots then became a hurricane late in the afternoon of July 9, with winds starting at sixty knots. Daniel reached its maximum intensity of a hundred knots (approx. 115 mph) peaking as a category 3 (major) hurricane early in the morning of July 11, a few hundred miles southwest of Manzanillo, Mexico. As the storm moved westward, it slowly weakened to a category 1 hurricane. Daniel regained tropical storm status during the night of July 14, entering the Central Basin as a weakening tropical storm on the morning of July 16. Daniel retained tropical storm intensity for the next few days before weakening into a tropical depression about 280 miles (450 km) south-southwest of the Big Island of Hawaii, being sheared by an upper trough. The depression then turned northward, and on July 22, dissipated in the Alenuihaha Channel between Maui and the Big Island of Hawaii. Duration July 7 – July 22, 1982.

While *Little Breeze* and I were not close to the center of Daniel (1400 nautical miles from the center on July 13, and only about 800 nautical miles from the center on July 16), hurricanes spread their fierce effects out for hundreds of miles. *Little Breeze* would have been (with that much open-ocean fetch) affected quite a bit by fairly rough seas and significant winds.

Little Breeze has performed beyond my expectations as a seagoing vessel as she sheltered me through those terrifying moments in the storms. My little boat has been my home both at sea and here in the islands.

Saturday
August 20, 1983

JOURNAL

I can't believe time has passed so quickly, I haven't written in my journal for eight months! My time is spent mostly working odd jobs, I am in funds again but none of this is the opportunity I was in search of. The long list of former employers is getting discouraging. I have cleaned carpets, bused tables, crewed on a shrimp trawler, worked on a parasail boat and did some work for Green Peace. On my own, I have at times taken passengers aboard *Little Breeze* and gone out for a day of whale watching and sailing around the islands.

The recession of 1982 hasn't helped much in terms of finding gainful employment. After spending over a year in Hawaii, the search for purpose and a life fulfilling vocation has not ended. Should I continue on trying to establish myself here on the islands or contemplate another change?

I ask myself what are my skills? I of course say sailing, but I'm not a great sailor. What are my talents and my aptitudes? I will continue my soul searching.

(This would be my last Journal entry.)

WHAT HAPPENS NEXT?

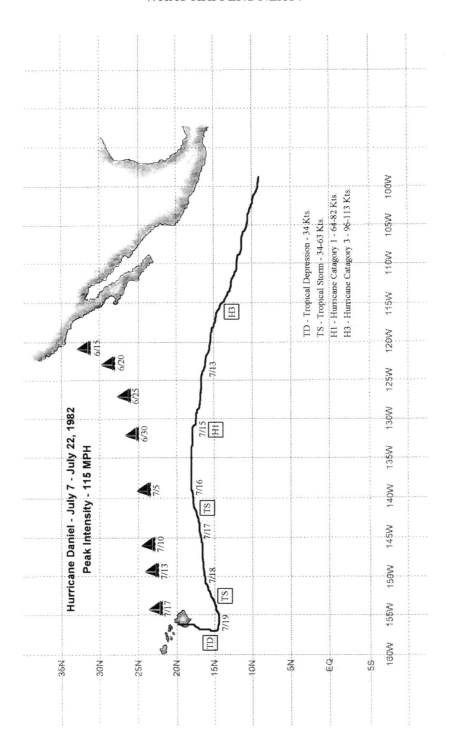

Epilogue

Not long after *Little Breeze* and I sailed into Lahaina, Maui, an old white steamer anchored off shore. That afternoon, I ran into a few of the steamer's midshipmen, walking about town in their crisp, starched, white uniforms, and soon learned they were from the California Maritime Academy. I was pretty curious as to who they were and struck up a conversation with some of them. They informed me they were attending a merchant marine academy in California, and were on a training cruise. "The Merchant Marine?" I asked, "What is that? Can you make any money?" They shared stories of the waterside campus on the northern end of San Francisco Bay and their expectations of becoming officers in the American Merchant Marine.

I soon spent four years at the California Maritime Academy (CMA) obtaining a Bachelor of Science degree in Nautical Industrial Technology, a Bachelor of Science degree in Marine Transportation Management, and obtained my United States Coast Guard Third Mate's License.

Before striking out on my new adventure at CMA, I sold my *Little Breeze* to Mr. Fran Burr, a bartender in Waikiki. He had seen my little three-by-five-inch 'For Sale' card tacked

EPILOGUE

on the Keehi Lagoon Harbor Master's bulletin board. Fran said he would buy my boat, full price, as long as I stayed in Hawaii until I could teach him how to sail. This took about two weeks and then I flew back to southern California, where I had started my voyage 2,260 miles and one-and-one-half years earlier. By November 1983 I was once again enrolled in Orange Coast College to bone up on my academic skills.

The young man who challenged the sea in his little Montgomery 15 has today come full circle.

When I sailed away from California on June 11, 1982 it meant I was leaving behind an uncertain future because at that time I had no idea what I was going to do with my life. I wanted the voyage over to the islands to open up new opportunities or at least point me in the right direction. Perhaps there was a glimmer of hope that Hawaii offered something new, maybe something I hadn't thought of before.

In total, I spent well over a year exhausting my search on the islands. In trying to prove myself while living the carefree island life, it become very apparent I was wasting time.

The providential encounter of meeting cadets from the maritime academy caused me to think differently about a seagoing career. It was much later that my dad would remind me he had suggested I consider enrolling in the California Maritime Academy following my high school graduation. But at that time I wasn't ready for the disciplined routine of academy life and I had no idea what the job opportunities would be. I had always considered my ability and love of sailing a hobby. Now I had finally come to realize that what I had been searching for was right under my nose the whole time!

EPILOGUE

All of the challenges, difficulties and obstacles I faced in accomplishing my voyage would be preparation for the academy and life at sea as a merchant seaman. The thirty-eight days with their solitude, the unpredictable daily environment and the discipline needed to stay focused on the task were all invaluable preparation for my future.

For many people their job is a constant source of boredom and frustration. I can truthfully say I find enjoyment in my profession. The shipping industry with its variety, its challenges and the ability for it to complement my family life is more than I had ever anticipated.

I have been a professional mariner for twenty-seven years, sailing as Third Mate, Second Mate, Chief Mate and Master aboard U.S. flag merchant vessels of different size and purpose. When I think back over those years my thoughts eventually return to those days and nights sailing to Hawaii on board the *Little Breeze*. God granted me the desire of my heart, and that was this: if I were to make it to Hawaii, I would find a school where I would be trained to become a professional mariner. Pretty ironic since after only nine days and 500 miles out of Long Beach I had written in my journal that the sailing on commercial ships didn't appeal to me.

Well my desire to sail professionally has come to pass. In the process, I have met many new challenges, sailed around the world, and, of course, met my wife, with whom I have spent twenty-six happily married years. In that time, I have been able to share my life at sea with my wife Laurie; many companies have allowed her to accompany me to a variety of foreign ports on various types of vessels. In 1995, she was on board with me during our seventh wedding anniversary. With Captain Marty Philips officiating, we renewed our marriage vows on the bow of the Liquid Natural Gas Carrier Louisiana, while anchored in the Persian Gulf with the entire crew in attendance. That was a first for everyone on board.

I have now sailed thousands of miles of oceans, spent many morning and evening watches gazing at the stars, witnessed many beautiful sunrises and sunsets, docked in ports all over the world, but I still think back to that fateful voyage that started it all.

I sailed out of Long Beach harbor in 1982 with only the bare essentials. I had no GPS, no mobile handheld satellite phone, no internet and no Skype; some of which were not yet available. *Little Breeze* had no portable generator, solar paneling or wind power generator to extend the life of my batteries. And of course *Little Breeze* did not have a water maker or an automatic pilot. When leaving my father's dock it was just me, the *Little Breeze* and a very unpredictable Pacific Ocean.

My solo voyage to Hawaii means a lot to me, especially the fact of doing everything, as much as I could, on my own. It was a great challenge and upon completion, a wonderful personal accomplishment.

I never considered enlisting sponsors because I wanted to answer only to myself and to have the freedom to make my own decisions. I never thought about publicity because I didn't want to bother with it. But now to publish my story, with much help and encouragement from my wife, and have others enjoy reading it, will be both a joy to me and a rewarding personal achievement for us both.

EPILOGUE

The only small boat sailing Laurie and I do now is with the Travis Presidio Yacht Club, sailing on San Francisco Bay.

For any reader that may be interested in what has become of *Little Breeze*, after many miles under her keel, she still sails the waters of the Hawaiian Islands and can be found on a Google search of Little Breeze Montgomery 15. *Little Breeze* is legendary and her story of the thirty-eight day voyage across the Pacific is told on Montgomery brochures, websites, and blogs and over the years has been repeated by an unknown number of Montgomery sailboat owners.

Renewing vows on the LNG Louisiana

Captain Marty Phillips officiating

Appendix I

The provisions and supplies on board at departure by LOCATION and by *container*

CENTER CABIN

Cans

3	Chili	*4*	Zucchini
5	Pork and beans	*3*	Green beans
3	Vegetable beef	*2*	Mixed vegetables
1	Ravioli	*1*	Split pea
2	Beef soup	*1*	Pineapple
1	Split pea and ham	*8*	Fruit cocktail
2	Cream of mushroom	*5*	Apple sauce
2	Chicken noodle	*6*	Pears
3	Cream of chicken	*3*	Peach
2	Refried beans	*2*	Pear nectar
1	Lasagna	*1*	Papaya nectar
1	Beef stew	*6*	Apple juice
3	Tuna	*7*	Condensed milk
1	Mexican bean	*1*	Box minute rice
7	Vienna sausage	*2*	Box instant mashed potatoes
8	Corn	*?*	Mystery can
4	Lima beans		

UNDER COCKPIT SOLE

24	Apple juice 6 oz.	*6*	Pineapple juice 6 oz.
8	Nectars	*4*	Velveeta cheese
12	Grapefruit juice 6 oz	*4*	Margarine

APPENDIX I

Yellow bag

1	Lasagna	4	Chili
2	Cream of chicken	2	Pork and beans
3	Split pea	2	Stew
3	Ravioli	1	Ham
1	Spaghetti	1	Mexican bean

White bucket

1	Ketchup	1	Green chilies
1	Minced onion	1	Hawaiian bread
1	Instant Coffee (jar)	3	Pam cooking spray
2	24 oz. bag of peanuts	18	Butane lighters
1	Teriyaki sauce	3	Butane fuel cans

Laundry bag

1	Lasagna	1	Pork and beans
7	Stew	4	Fruit cocktail
2	Spaghetti	1	Pears
1	Beef soup	4	Pineapple
1	Cream of mushroom	2	Peach
1	Ham		

Misc. stuffed all over

30	Top Ramen	1	Funnel
3	Hawaiian bread	2	Shampoo
100	Tea bags	2	Thermoses
2	Jelly		Bag of books
1	Pepper	1	Trash bags (box)
1	Salt		Misc. Clothing
1	Liter coke	1	Anchor
2	Peanut butter		All the jibs

APPENDIX I

STARBOARD CABIN LOCKER

2	Eggs (dozen)	*1*	Garlic salt
6	Pinapple juice	*25*	Instant oatmeal
1	Tang	*3*	Rice-A-Roni (boxes)
1	Minced onions	*1*	Mustard
2	Pam cooking spray	*1*	Bisquick
24	Granola bars	*1*	Instant Coffee (jar)
6	Pineapple juice	*1*	Honey
1	Ketchup		Misc. Cooking utensils
1	Tabasco Sauce	*4*	Butane fuel canisters

FORWARD CABIN LOCKER

2   12-volt car batteries

Brown sack

1	Bisquick	*1*	Minute rice
3	Pam cooking spray	*2*	Boston beans
3	Bread		Misc. lines
1	Uncle Ben's Rice		

APPENDIX I

WATER
(stored in combination of 1 liter soda and 1 gallon chlorine bottles)

gallons	Location
8	Under forward locker
3 ½	Starboard locker
3	Port locker
11	Under cockpit
4	In footwell
5	In cockpit

CLOTHING

10	Short sleeve shirts	3	Watch caps
6	T-shirts	6	Long pants
6	Sweat shirts	5	Long underwear
10	Long sleeved shirts	2	Belts
6	Short pants	1	Atlantis foul weather gear
3	Bathing suits	2	Wool gloves
6	Boxer shorts	3	Scarves
4	Towels	2	Tennis shoes
1	Light jacket	12	Socks (pair)

TOILETRIES

1	Hand lotion	1	Talcum powder
1	Suntan lotion	1	Sunscreen
1	Nail clippers	2	Mirrors
4	Toilet tissue (rolls)	2	Dental floss
4	Shampoo	1	Comb
2	Tooth paste	1	Brush

APPENDIX I

FIRST AID KIT

Band aids (all sizes)	Adhesive tape
Cotton balls	Gauze
Surgical tape	Sterile pads
Alcohol	Burn ointment
Ace bandage	Eye drops
Desenex foot powder	Maalox
Tylenol	Alka-Seltzer
Q-tips	Benadryl 50mg
Vibra-Tabs 100mg	

GALLEY EQUIPMENT

1	Forespar gimbaled marine stove	*2*	Thermos
20	Propane fuel (cans)	*2*	Cooking pots
1	Sterno stove (camping type for backup)	*2*	Bowls
10	Sterno fuel (cans)	*2*	Plates
15	Disposable lighters	*3*	Cups
1	Spatula	*2*	Knives
8	Paper towels (rolls)	*2*	Forks
2	Manuel can openers	*2*	Spoons
3	Army type can openers	*1*	Measuring cups (set)
		1	Water dispenser with pump action

TOOLS

1	Hand drill (w/bits)	*1*	Tape measure
1	Small crowbar	*1*	Scissors
2	Files	*1*	Wire cutters
2	Knives	*2*	Crescent wrenches
5	Screw drivers (various sizes)	*2*	Putty knives
2	Pliers	*2*	C clamps
2	Vice grips		

APPENDIX I

MISCELLANEOUS

2	Masking tape (rolls)	*1*	Duct tape
1	Electrical tape	*2*	Silicon sealer tubes
2	Dolphinite tubes	*2*	WD-40 (cans)
6	Bungee cords (various sizes)	*4*	Sponges
6	Plastic trash bags (medium)	*4*	Whipping line (spools)
5	Sewing needles	*1*	Small plastic tarp
1	Electrical wire	*3*	Buckets

SPARE PARTS

4	Flashlight bulbs	*1*	Shroud cable
12	AA batteries	*6*	Waterproof matches (boxes)
16	C batteries	*12*	Cotter pins
12	D batteries	*12*	Shear pins
12	Split rings	*1*	Spare line (yacht braid 1/4" x 100')
10	Blocks (various sizes)	*1*	Tiller jaws (set)
1	Rudder rod (Provided by Montgomery)	*6*	Cable clamps

ANCHOR GEAR

2 pound Bruce

4.4 pound Bruce

300' x 5/16 inch yacht braid

30' x 5/16 inch galvanized chain

150' x ¼ inch yacht braid

20' x ¼ inch galvanized chain

3 hp British Seagull outboard motor on stern
(with only the ½ gallon of gas in tank)

APPENDIX II

NAVIGATION EQUIPMENT

Compasses
(2 Danforth bulkhead mount in cockpit and Airguide inside cabin as telltale)
Sextant – Davis Mach-15
Calculator
Timex watch
Casio chronometer watch (bought at Kmart for $19.95)
Paraglide protractor plotter
Binoculars (Bushnell 7x35)
VDO SumLog
Time Cube (from Radio Shack)
Life Harness
Channel Island Charts
North Pacific Chart
Hawaiian Island Charts
Pilot Charts (June, July, August)
Light list
Nautical Almanac
H.O. – 249

MISC. EQUIPMENT

1	Small Rubber Raft w/oars	*1*	Fire extinguisher
1	Radar reflector	*1*	Strobe flashlight
1	Distress signal flares, smoke and water dye	*1*	VHF Radio (hand held)
2	Flashlights	*1*	Life Jacket
		1	Tape Recorder

Appendix III

Estimated Costs and Donations
(for equipment and supplies)

    $50 Clothing
    $30 Toiletries
    $40 First aid
  $435 Sails
  $200 Structural and Rigging
  $720 Equipment
  $300 Food

EQUIPMENT AND SUPPLIES DONATED BY

Mom – Hand Held VHF Radio

Dad – Sweat shirts, pants, socks, food, and antibiotics

Whitney Marshman – pre-recorded music cassettes

Marc Hightower – Storm jib, water containers, spare rigging, drain plugs, and the use of house and tools

Jerry Montgomery – Material for running backstays, bottom paint, tools, material, masthead tricolor, rudder bar, and tiller jaws

Stan Susman – Anchor and line, flare kit, tape recorder, strobe flashlight, socks, and a *lot of advice.*

Appendix IV

Little Breeze Recipes

Rolled Biscuits
2 cups Bisquick mix
2/3 cup milk
Or if using water
2 ½ cups Bisquick mix
2/3 cup of water
Beat vigorously for 30 seconds
Turn onto cloth covered board that is well dusted with mix
Knead 10 minutes, put biscuits in pot, cover and bake until done

Mashed Potatoes
¾ cup water
1 tablespoon margarine
¼ teaspoon salt
Bring to a boil and add
¼ cup milk
¾ cup instant potato flakes
Stir until fluffy

Uncle Ben's Rice
Bring 2 ½ cups of water to a boil
Stir in
1 cup rice
1 teaspoon salt
1 tablespoon margarine
Simmer for 20 minutes
Remove from heat and let stand 3 minutes

Minute Rice
¾ cup water (Less water for firmer rice or add a full can of cream soup)
Bring water to a boil and add in:
¾ cup rice
¼ teaspoon salt
1 tablespoon margarine (Let stand 5 to 10 minutes)

GLOSSARY OF NAUTICAL TERMS

Aft – The portion of the vessel behind the middle area of the vessel.

Advancing lines of position – A line of position which has been moved forward along the course line to allow for the run since the line was established.

Backstay – A rope or cable extending from the top of a mast aft to a vessel's side or stern to help support the mast.

Ballast – Heavy weight built into the bottom of the keel of the vessel to increase stability.

Bare Pole – The condition of a sailing vessel when she has no sail set.

Becalmed – Lying adrift for lack of wind to power the sails.

Bend (Bent) – To affix or tie-off.

Bilge pump – Removes accumulated water from the lowest portion of the vessel.

Boom - The horizontal spar to which the foot of a fore & aft sail is attached.

Broached – To be thrown broadside into a trough out of control.

Broad Reaching – The boat is sailing away from the wind, but not directly downwind.

Broadside – The entire side of a ship above the waterline.

Celestial Navigation – navigation by means of observations made of the apparent position of heavenly bodies.

Chronometer – A timekeeper accurate enough to be used to determine longitude by means of celestial navigation.

Cleat – A deck fitting of metal or wood, having opposing horns around which a line is secured.

GLOSSARY

Clew – The lower aft corner of a fore and aft sail, or the lower corner at the foot of a square sail.

Close reaching – A point of sail where the boat is sailing towards the wind.

Coaming – A raised partition around the cockpit of small sailboats which keeps water from entering the cockpit well.

Cockpit – An open well aft in a small sailboat at which the helmsman sits to steer.

Companionway – A stepped passageway used to go from one deck to another.

Cuddy cabin – A very small cabin usually affording only sitting headroom on a small sailboat or launch.

Dead Reckoning (DR) – A method of navigating by calculating a position using the course, speed and time from a known position or fix.

Dead Astern – Directly aft.

Drop boards – A segment of two or three sections of teak planks that shut the companionway. The bottom one comes up to the gunwales and is generally good enough to block most of the water out of the cockpit in case swamped.

Emergency Position Indicating Radio Beacon (EPIRB) – Distress radio tracking transmitters which aid in the detection and location of boats.

Fix – A determination of the exact location of a ship by bearings or celestial calculations.

Fore – Towards the bow of the vessel.

Forestay – The cable or line in the standing rigging which runs from the head of the foremost mast to the foredeck at the bow.

Genoa sail – A large foresail that reaches aft past the mast and overlaps the mainsail.

Ghosted – To sail along very slowly when there appears to be no wind.

Gimbal – A pivoted device that suspends a compass, stove or other devise so that it remains level when its support is tilted.

Gunnel or Gunwale – The top edge on the side of the boat.

Halyard – Any of various lines or tackles for hoisting a spar, sail, flag, etc., into position for use.

Heave To – To stop a boat and maintain position (with some leeway) by balancing rudder and sail to prevent forward movement, a boat stopped this way is "hove to"; such as when in heavy seas. The idea is to bring the wind onto the weather bow and hold the ship in that position, where she can safely and easily ride out a storm.

High Altitude Sight (Arc of Position) – This line of position is a circle having the geographical position as its center and a radius equal to the zenith distance. This method is normally used only for bodies at high altitudes, having small zenith distances.

Jib – A foresail, a triangle shaped sail forward of the mast that does not reach aft of the mast.

Jibe or Gybe – To change a ship's course to make the boom shift sides.

Knot – A unit of speed over the water of one nautical mile per hour.

Lapstrake – Referring to a wooden boat built with overlapping planks. The fastenings are rivets or clench nails.

Latitude – One of the two coordinates (the other being longitude) used to locate a position at sea; marked in degrees north or south of the equator, from 0 degrees at the equator to 90 degrees north or south at the poles; one degree of latitude = 60 minutes of latitude; as one minute equals a mile, a common saying at sea is "a minute's a mile". Latitude is comparable to the x-axis on a graph.

GLOSSARY

Leech – After or trailing edge of a sail; the after edge of a fore-and-aft sail and the outer edges of a square sail.

Leeway – 1) Measurement of movement of a vessel to the side opposite the wind. 2) The amount of navigable seaway available to the lee of a vessel.

Line of Position (LOP) –- may be derived from celestial observations or observation of terrestrial objects whose location is known.

Line of sight – The straight line between two points.

List - The leaning of a boat to the side because of excess weight on that side; inclination of a boat due to excess weight on one side or the other.

Longitude – One of the two coordinates (the other being latitude) used to locate a position at sea; marked in degrees east or west of the prime meridian (0 degrees longitude) universally accepted to be at Greenwich, England. As there are 360 degrees in a circle, longitude may range up to 180 degrees East or West. 180 degrees East and West meet on the other side of the globe from Greenwich, at the International Date Line.

Magnetic – Magnetic course – A course relative to magnetic north.

Meridian – The meridian used for reckoning zone time; this is generally the nearest meridian whose longitude is exactly divisible by 15°.

Most Probable Position (MPP) – Is that position of a craft judged to be most accurate when an element of doubt exists as to the true position.

Nautical Mile – One minute of latitude; approximately 6076 feet - about 1/8 longer than the statute mile of 5280 feet.

Plot - To plan a direction of travel by marking a chart and taking

GLOSSARY

into consideration all the variables such as the speed of the boat, winds, currents, tides, water depth, hazards, markers and time.

Pooped – Swamped by a high, following sea.

Radar Reflector – A device designed to reflect radar waves well in order to make it clearly visible on radar screens of other vessels.

Reef – The shortening of a sail in heavy winds by securing the lower portion at its reef points thereby reducing the power of the sail and the part of a sail that is folded under when it is shortened.

Rig – Rigging – The system of masts and lines on ships and other sailing vessels.

Running Fix - Rfx - A navigational fix obtained by using a line of position (LOP) taken at or near the current time together with another, earlier LOP that has been advanced for the movement of the vessel between these two times.

Sail – A large piece of fabric designed to be hoisted on the spars of a sailboat in such a manner as to catch the wind and propel the boat.

Sea Anchor – A device used to stabilize a boat in heavy weather. The sea anchor increases the drag through the water and thus acts as a brake.

Sextant – A precision instrument used to measure the elevation of celestial bodies above the horizon as a means of determining the position of the ship.

Sheet – A line leading from the lee corner of a sail or the end of a boom and used to control the angle of the sail to the wind.

Spar – A pole used as part of the sailboat rigging, such as masts, booms, gaffs, yards, etc. A vertical spar is a mast.

Starboard Quarter – The sides of a vessel aft of amidships; i.e., port quarter or starboard quarter.

Stern – The after part of the boat.

GLOSSARY

Strobe Light – A device used to produce regular flashes of light and is used for anti-collision lighting.

Sun Sight – An observation of the altitude of the sun made for navigational purposes.

Swell – A formation of long-wavelength surface waves.

Tack – To change course by turning into and through the eye of the wind so that the wind comes from the other side of the boat. To come about.

Thwart – A seat or brace fastened from gunwale to gunwale in a small boat or canoe to keep the shape and add strength.

Tiller – A long hand lever attached to the top of the rudder, used to steer the vessel.

Toe-rail – A low strip running around the edge of the deck like a low bulwark. It may be shortened or have gaps in it to allow water to flow off the deck.

Trades or Trade Winds – Persistent tropical winds that blow westward and toward the Equator. They are stronger and more consistent over the oceans than over land. Their average speed is about 8 to 11 knots (11 to 13 miles per hour) but can increase to speeds of 26 knots (30 miles per hour) or more. The trade winds blow predominantly from the northeast in the Northern Hemisphere and from the southeast in the Southern Hemisphere, strengthening during the winter and at times when the air pressure is high over the poles.

Transom – The flat outboard stern structure of a ship from keel to deck.

Trough – The depression between two waves.

Turnbuckles – A mechanism with a threaded opening at both ends which connects to a shroud or stay, and by turning closed, draws the ends together and puts tension on the gear.

Twin Headsails – Two specially designed jibs attached to the forestay.

Variation – Magnetic variation. The difference, east or west, between magnetic north and true north, measured as an angle. Magnetic variation varies in different geographic locations.

Veer – To have the wind shift in a clockwise direction

Warp – A method of holding a boat against the wind using a sea anchor.

Weather Helm – A tendency of a vessel with poorly trimmed sails to continually turn upwind.

Whisker Pole – A light spar which holds the jib out away from the mast when sailing downwind.

Made in the USA
San Bernardino, CA
11 May 2016